Reading Minds
and Markets

Reading Minds and Markets

Minimizing Risk and Maximizing Returns
in a Volatile Global Marketplace

Jack Ablin

Chief Investment Officer,
Harris Private Bank

with Suzanne McGee

Contributing Editor, Barron's

Vice President, Publisher: Tim Moore
Associate Publisher and Director of Marketing: Amy Neidlinger
Executive Editor: Jim Boyd
Editorial Assistants: Myesha Graham and Pamela Boland
Development Editor: Russ Hall
Operations Manager: Gina Kanouse
Senior Marketing Manager: Julie Phifer
Publicity Manager: Laura Czaja
Assistant Marketing Manager: Megan Colvin
Cover Designer: Roberto de Vicq de Cumptich
Managing Editor: Kristy Hart
Project Editor: Betsy Harris
Copy Editor: Keith Cline
Proofreader: Williams Woods Publishing Services
Senior Indexer: Cheryl Lenser
Compositor: Jake McFarland
Manufacturing Buyer: Dan Uhrig

© 2009 by Pearson Education, Inc.
Publishing as FT Press
Upper Saddle River, New Jersey 07458

This book is sold with the understanding that neither the author nor the publisher is engaged in rendering legal, accounting or other professional services or advice by publishing this book. Each individual situation is unique. Thus, if legal or financial advice or other expert assistance is required in a specific situation, the services of a competent professional should be sought to ensure that the situation has been evaluated carefully and appropriately. The author and the publisher disclaim any liability, loss, or risk resulting directly or indirectly, from the use or application of any of the contents of this book.

The views and opinions expressed in this book are those of the authors only and are not to be attributed to Harris N.A. or its parent company, Bank of Montreal, or any of their subsidiaries, affiliates, employees, directors or officers (collectively, "Harris"). Harris does not endorse or support the views or opinions set forth in this book. The authors alone are responsible for the accuracy and reliability of any performance numbers provided in this book. Past performance is no guarantee of future results. This book is not intended to constitute investment advice with respect to any particular security or basket of securities. Harris is not responsible in any manner for direct, indirect, special or consequential damages, howsoever caused, arising out of reliance on the information contained in this book.

FT Press offers excellent discounts on this book when ordered in quantity for bulk purchases or special sales. For more information, please contact U.S. Corporate and Government Sales, 1-800-382-3419, corpsales@pearsontechgroup.com. For sales outside the U.S., please contact International Sales at international@pearson.com.

Printed in the United States of America

Second Printing Septemer 2009

ISBN-10: 0-13-235497-7

ISBN-13: 978-0-13-235497-4

Pearson Education LTD.

Pearson Education Australia PTY, Limited.

Pearson Education Singapore, Pte. Ltd.

Pearson Education North Asia, Ltd.

Pearson Education Canada, Ltd.

Pearson Educación de Mexico, S.A. de C.V.

Pearson Education—Japan

Pearson Education Malaysia, Pte. Ltd.

The Library of Congress Cataloging-in-Publication data is on file.

I dedicate this book to LeeAnn,
Elise, Emily, and Lynne Ablin.
—Jack

Contents

Acknowledgments

I would like to acknowledge the great effort and inspiration offered by my colleagues at Harris Private Bank, including Terry Jenkins, Graham Parsons, Brent Schutte, Jeffery Weniger, Jose Santillan, and Maria Garcia; the professionals at Ned Davis Research and Bloomberg; and my clients and professional associates who make this business a stimulating and rewarding experience.

—Jack Ablin

I owe a debt of gratitude to Jack Ablin for entrusting me with this project and for his patience as I worked to translate his ideas into prose—I hope the result does justice to his methodology. Thanks also to Jim Boyd at FT Press for his patience with the sometimes arduous process. Friends and family helped keep me sane; thanks in particular to Elizabeth Wine and Glenn Becker.

—Suzanne McGee

About the Authors

Jack Ablin is an Executive Vice President and Chief Investment Officer for Harris Private Bank in Chicago. With more than 25 years of experience in the investment business, Mr. Ablin was a mortgage-backed securities trader, a fund manager as well as a Director of Investments. He served in the Finance Department in the School of Management at Boston University and was the President of the Boston Security Analysts Society. Jack makes his home in Chicago with his wife, LeeAnn, and daughters, Elise and Emily.

Suzanne McGee has spent more than two decades writing about business and finance, including 13 years at the *Wall Street Journal* in Toronto, New York, and London. She is currently a contributing editor at *Barron's* and a regular contributor to *Institutional Investor*. Her work has appeared in the *Financial Times*, *INC*, *Art + Auction*, and the *New York Post*. She is a recipient of both a Gerald Loeb Award and SABEW's Best in Business Award. Suzanne lives in Brooklyn, where she is now at work on a book about Wall Street.

1

The Year of Investing Dangerously

The odds are that a few decades from now, when I've retired from the business of managing money—and if I'm still alive—young money managers will ask me, with awe, what it was like to be a professional investor during the Great Financial Markets Meltdown of 2008.

I already know what my answer will be. It was a nightmare—and the ultimate challenge to any investor and any investment strategy, including me and mine. When the first signs of real trouble appeared in 2007, culminating in the collapse of Bear Stearns and its last-ditch purchase by J.P. Morgan, most of us figured that we were experiencing the worst that another economic and market cycle could deliver. This, we all figured, was just another bump in the road of long-term progress. Having lived through the stock market crash of 1987, the recession of the early 1990s, and the dot.com market meltdown, I thought I understood what market turmoil was all about. But then, in the space of only a few months in the second half of 2008, the entire rule book had to be rewritten or just tossed into the garbage. Every tried-and-true tactic failed. Diversification? Forget it—when one market slumped, every other market followed suit, and logic be damned. Even gold, which is supposed to be the most resilient asset of all, the one that everyone flocks to own when they think Armageddon is only hours away, failed to behave as expected. When stock markets plunged and the credit markets entered a deep freeze—at the height of the irrationality—the price of gold plunged 30%. The conviction that downturns were simply opportunities in disguise for the savvy investor vanished almost overnight: Buying on the dips and holding for the recovery didn't work. There was no recovery; the losses just got larger. No wonder the events of 2008 called into question every iota of conventional wisdom about investing.

Looking back, I suspect that in retrospect we all will see 2008 as an inflection point, after which many professional investors went back to—or were kicked back to—the drawing board. It is now clear to everyone that investing isn't just about identifying and seizing opportunities to earn the maximum possible return, but also about identifying and avoiding risks that could catastrophically impact portfolios. The conventional wisdom can be wrong—and I don't think the old rules are going to apply again, or at least not for a long time to come. Going forward, we, along with every other investor out there, will be working in a new environment, one with far more headwinds than tailwinds. However, our most recent experience should not call into question why we invest in the market, but rather it should serve as a lesson that investing is not easy. Investing takes hard work, consistency, and objectivity.

When I'm asked decades from now how I managed to survive the events of 2008 and its aftermath, the answer will be easy: my investment methodology. Indeed, I ended the year feeling particularly fortunate. That might sound strange in the circumstances—after all, the portfolios that we run for clients at Harris Private Bank ended up in the red in 2008, like those of almost every other diversified money manager. (Only 1 of 1,700 or so diversified funds with more than $50 million in assets and at least a 3-year track record managed to post a positive return in 2008: and that fund accomplished the feat only on the last trading day of the year.) Going into 2008, our all-equity strategy had been doing better than a majority of comparably positioned mutual fund managers.

Unfortunately, 2008 turned out to be one of those years that no one could cope with. It was the worst year for stocks since 1931—during the height of the Great Depression—and the fact that our equity-oriented strategies outperformed the S&P 500 that year was, of course, no comfort to anyone because the S&P 500 itself plunged

38.5%. There is no possible consolation for losing that much of your investors' money. Still, some outperformance was a faint glimmer of hope that we had managed to read the warning signs correctly—although we hadn't anticipated the sheer magnitude of the down-turn—and we had been able to react relatively promptly.

That's the nature of the world of professional money managers. Despite an awful year for the market, we were confident that we could navigate effectively within our investment policies. Still, at the beginning of 2008, I was worried. Two-thirds of U.S. economists were willing to believe that the United States would manage to avoid a recession that year, according to a January poll by the *Wall Street Journal*; Wall Street analysts were calling for a 16% jump in corporate profits. My own convictions, formed after "reading the market's mind" in the shape of the data, disputed conventional wisdom. I believed we were headed for a recession; already, by January, year over year we had seen a 30% plunge in investment in private purchases of residential real estate, only one of many red flags. At best, I figured, companies in the S&P 500 might end up seeing profits *fall* by 5% in 2008. (As of this writing in early 2009, actual earnings for the year were shaping up to be nearly 20% lower than 2007 levels.)

What all that tells me today is that the more we responded to the signals the market was sending, the greater was our degree of outper-formance. We lost less—a great deal less—than we would have if we hadn't been paying attention to those signals at all. Sure, you can't eat relative return, as the Wall Street cliché goes, but given a choice between losing nearly 40 percent and a return that was somewhat insulated from that erosion, I know which I would choose. And I am more confident than ever that the data-based strategy I have been developing and using for decades is the methodology best suited to navigating this new, hostile investment environment.

That's a bold assertion, I realize, especially since I'm writing this in the early months of 2009, with my losses still fresh in my mind and the markets still in turmoil. But the financial markets of the twenty-first century have so far shown themselves to be best navigable by those who are willing to look down at them from 30,000 feet. Those who insist on taking only a bottom-up view have often been caught off guard in the choppy and highly-volatile markets that have characterized the past few years. They're also trapped in a crowded market; by the end of 2007, according to PerTrac Financial Solutions, there were an astonishing 15,000 single-manager hedge funds and 7,400 funds of hedge funds (funds that invest in a diversified group of hedge funds, hoping to reduce volatility or risk) out there, all looking for the single best market idea—oil services stocks, perhaps, or bleeding-edge biotechnology businesses. Add these folks to the already overcrowded mutual fund arena, throw in the impact of new communication technologies that permit knowledge to zap from one part of the globe to another in nanoseconds, and you're looking at a *hyper*competitive environment.

Add to that the fact that all of us are now struggling to deal with a surreal degree of volatility, which in turn masks the fact that over the past decade most stock indexes have generated no lasting returns. Anyone who put $10,000 into the S&P 500 on January 1, 1998 and reinvested all of their dividends would have seen their portfolio value swell to $12,601 by August 2000, drop to $6,967 by September 2002, and then rebound and surge to a peak value of $14,509 by October 2007. But as of this writing, in early 2009, their $10,000 investment is worth a mere $8,699, an annualized *loss* of −1.38%.

When markets are that volatile, it's vital that investors find a way to earn an incremental return over and above what the indexes can deliver, at a reasonable cost, and without taking on much incremental risk. At the same time, trying to outsmart the market, everyone has always told you, is perilous. Unless, that is, you turn everything you know about investing on its head, as I am about to suggest to you in the pages of this book. Unless you learn to read the market's mind....

Forget about looking only for stock picks and chasing the hot concept of the day. Forget about the argument that you should just buy and hold and never worry about what I call tactical asset allocation and what critics dismissively label "market timing." Only if you try to approach the entire investment menu, from soup to nuts, and measure the relative risk and return of each item, can you begin to make rational decisions about your investment portfolio, especially in the post-2008 environment. And by being prepared to respond in a timely way to signals that the relative risks and return potential of each of those asset classes and categories have changed, you can generate incremental return. It's that incremental return, I am convinced, that will spell the difference between outperforming your peers and the market benchmarks and trailing miserably behind.

I have spent much of the past two decades or so developing or refining this methodology, one that is generally referred to in the investment world as a global macro strategy based on "quantitative" models (in other words, relying on the data to tell me which of many global asset classes I should be investing in). Each year, access to data has become simpler, thanks to new technologies and new products. Like all the best investment strategies, it has now become straightforward enough that I felt I could write this book; that I could spell out to you, the reader, how you can apply it to your own portfolios. You can count your net worth in tens of thousands of dollars rather than tens of millions of dollars—and, thanks to the democratizing impact of low-cost investment vehicles such as exchange-traded funds and the Internet communication revolution, any investor inclined to do it himself can use the same investment process that I do sitting in my office in Chicago as a professional money manager.

I believe market selection is far and away the most important investment decision that I can make for my clients and you can make on your own behalf. Numerous studies have shown that the markets in which you have exposure, whether they are stocks, bonds, real estate, or commodities, explain the overwhelming majority of how you

ultimately achieve your investment return. Therefore, asset allocation, both long term and opportunistic, is paramount in developing an
investment portfolio. However, once proper market allocations are
determined, investors must then decide how best to gain exposure to
those markets. There is a panoply of possible courses of action.
Whether you employ exchange-traded funds, mutual funds, or individual security selection to flesh out their investment portfolios is up
to you. The key to a successful portfolio is the underlying skeleton
that's both structurally sound and flexible. The global macro process
laid out in this book will help you construct and maintain that foundation. It's also as simple to use as if you were driving a car and keeping
an eye on the dashboard while still looking out the window and monitoring what is going on in your rear-view mirror. If you can successfully navigate the traffic on an interstate, adjusting to changes in
speed of traffic around you, what your fuel gauge is telling you and
the behavior of the lunatic driver of a tractor-trailer in the next lane,
you can navigate the financial markets using the series of quantitative
tools, or factors, that I outline for you here.

We live in challenging times, and even more now than when I
started working on this book in 2007. Soaring energy costs have crip-
pled the airline and automobile industries as well as giant chemical producers like DuPont. (True, oil prices, as I write this, are well below their
June 2008 peak of $148 a barrel, but they are also still well above their
2000 level of $28 a barrel.) Government regulations cost companies still
more; Sarbanes-Oxley alone, put in place to combat corporate malfeasance of the kind that destroyed Enron and WorldCom, their employees, and shareholders, costs the average U.S. company $2 million a year
to comply with. Hedge funds, already dumping their holdings into the
stock market as they slash the amount of leverage on their balance
sheets, are likely to be a target of new regulations, as are financial institutions. (My point isn't that regulation is a bad idea, but rather that
"good" and "bad" regulations alike carry with them costs, and those
costs eat into corporate profits and, ultimately, into investment returns.)

Above all, despite talk of a "peace dividend" in the 1990s in the wake of the collapse of the Berlin Wall and then the Soviet Union, we're back in a period of intense geopolitical conflict. The September 11 terrorist attacks ignited a costly "war on terror" by the United States and its allies, and two wars in Afghanistan and Iraq are draining billions of dollars from our government's coffers every month. Defending the nation is necessary, but it's also proving to be very costly; meanwhile, the geopolitical turmoil simply exacerbates the volatility of financial markets.

I'm not trying to tell our nation's policy makers what they should do next. My job is to find ways to outperform financial markets at a time when that task has been made more complex by what the policy makers are up to—and what they may do in the coming years. Like poker players (at least, like honest poker players who don't cheat), investors have no control whatsoever over what cards we are dealt. All we can do is make the most of whatever hand we are given. In poker, it's possible for a skilled player with an inferior hand to outwit and thus outplay someone with three kings. In investing, your odds of generating respectable incremental returns even in the most oppressive investment environment are better if you play your cards right.

Whether you're an individual investor or a pro, there are a myriad of ways to manage money; from buy and hold to point and click. Regardless of your approach, my mission in writing this book is to help individual investors gain a foothold in a fiercely competitive investment marketplace. If you're an experienced player, I'm hopeful that you'll be able to incorporate my process into your investment decision making. If you're new to the investment world, perhaps these steps will help you develop your own style. My own approach to doing this is *not* a get-rich-quick scheme. In fact, I hope that one of the reasons that you picked up this book is that you are just as sick of all those ridiculous and unrealistic promises of effortless ways to earn fabulous wealth as I am. To successfully outperform the market over the long term (not just overnight), you need to learn how to read the market's mind, to figure out where the risks and rewards are most acute at any given point in time. I'll introduce you to a set of metrics that will help you do just that. Some may be familiar—the price/earnings ratio, for instance, is a classic valuation technique. Others are likely to be more novel, such as the key role that monitoring the 200-day moving average of any market's index can play in your decision to jump in or out, pocketing profits and dodging dangers. Collectively, they represent a set of investment decision-making tools that you can use in whatever way you see fit, aggressively or defensively, depending on your own goals, liquidity needs, and risk tolerance. Each tool on its own is not an investment panacea, yet taken collectively, they provide a valuable mosaic of the investment landscape.

In my role as chief investment officer at Harris Private Bank, my team and I use the model and the tools I describe in this book every day of the week. We scrutinize each of the data points that I suggest you heed, and we put them into our investment dashboard, adjusting our direction, speed, and so on in response to the signals they send. How I drive the car when I'm the only passenger, how I drive it when it is full of a whole bunch of passengers all with different tolerances for speed, and how you will choose to drive it are all very different matters. In my role at Harris, I'm responsible for a busload of passengers, all of whom are very different and have different needs and objectives. Harris Private Bank, a division of Harris NA, has thousands of clients representing individuals and families with needs and objectives as varied as the families themselves. So, my ability to respond to the signals on my investment dashboard is determined to some extent by the fact that an aggressive response, although it might be perfectly acceptable to a handful of my clients who have specifically spelled out their investment desires, may be much too risky for many others. That's the essence of what is required of a professional investment manager devising model portfolios for clients based upon their individual risk tolerance; like my peers, I'm what is called a "trusted advisor." That's why our clients each have their own portfolio manager, an investment professional who customizes a strategy to serve their specific investment needs. When I refer to "my clients" or "Harris clients," I'm speaking in general terms and I do not intend to describe all our clients collectively. Within a broader investment process at Harris, my team and I serve as a critical resource for our portfolio managers. Those men and women, armed with their own impressive resumes, take the information our team supplies and, considering their clients' needs and proclivities, construct tailored portfolios. A triple-weight in emerging market equities can be great when the market is surging, but it's not for everyone. As long as you are honest with yourself about your own needs, goals, and risk tolerance, you can employ these tools any way you want. You can be as aggressive as the most ferocious hedge fund manager, responding to the data signals about markets that you receive by shorting some markets and buying call options on other securities. Or you can use the same tools in the most conservative portfolio, to tell you when it's time to move another 2% of your cash holdings back into stocks. Regardless of the way you choose to use this information, it will help you make more confident decisions.

We may not encounter the outsize volatility and horrific investment losses that characterized 2008 for another decade or longer. But in the investment environment we must navigate in the wake of that agonizing market climate, all of us need to be able to respond to market signals as accurately and rapidly as possible to capture each smidgen of investment income we can find. In the pages that follow, I show you exactly how to do so—and how to avoid the traps that can eat into that return.

2

The World of Global Macro

Once every 4 months or so, an invitation arrives in the mail and I find myself on a plane to one warm and sunny destination or another to deliver a speech at one of the country's biggest investment extravaganzas, the Money Show. These presentations tend to follow a pattern. I'll tell a roomful of eager-to-learn investors what broad trends I see taking shape. Every year, the specific questions change—as 2008 dawned, for instance, they revolved around the real estate crisis and the looming credit crunch—but inevitably someone will ask me the secret of picking those investments that are about to outperform the rest. In other words, they're searching for the investment equivalent of the Holy Grail.

I sympathize with my listeners, who are struggling to learn everything they need to know about how to manage their own portfolios. They'll try to cram in a dizzying array of workshops and panel discussions into the 4-day-long conference, ranging in nature from the mundane to the esoteric. How to choose among such offerings as "Investing in China through Taiwan" and "Zinc Opportunities on the Pacific Rim"? One recent show in Orlando featured an astonishing 320 workshops and 20 panel discussions. As if that wasn't enough, the exhibition hall, with a dazzling array of 250 or so exhibitors, would have satisfied any curious investor's need to know.

Those exhibit halls give me a chance to see, firsthand, just what the average investor is up against. Take a look at this new mutual fund, one company pleads. Put your business card in the big jar over here and win a free copy of the latest "Get Rich in 90 Days" tome, or the newest investment software, another urges. Attendees are bombarded with new products from one end of the vast exhibition hall to the other. Interested in Web 2.0? There is someone on hand to explain how he can help you identify the best stock picks in the sector. Those leaving a seminar during which pundits argued that commodity prices may be in the midst of a sustained bull market are likely to find, just outside the door, a table displaying examples of a commodity-investing newsletter. Subscribe for only $125, the sign above it promises, and you'll get a year's worth of tips about penny mining stocks. The trendier an investment theme and the more a market's valuation has soared, the more dollars investment firms of all stripes devote to promoting it. What else can explain the recent prominence at Money Fairs of exhibitors devoted to Canadian energy trusts, gold-linked investment vehicles or—before the 2007/2008 market crash—real estate investment trusts (REITs)?

This phenomenon is hardly new. For the past four centuries or so, ever since men and women began investing their hard-earned capital in ventures ranging from the spice trade to the development of new windmills, there have been folks eager to advise them on just how to go about that unfamiliar process. Through the years, product offerings have expanded to accommodate the investing public. But over the past two or three decades, the array of asset classes available to the average investor has skyrocketed. At the same time, companies began to shift the burden of investing for retirement from the corporate treasurer to the individual employee by switching from defined benefit to defined contribution retirement plans. Whether or not 401(k) plan participants were fascinated by investing, they found themselves having to learn about it—or suffer the consequences. This transition occurred nearly simultaneously with the globalization of the world economy and the information technology revolution, both of which made a greater array of new investment products more viable and easier to construct and manage. These days, if you can dream of a niche investment arena (Montenegrin real estate? Scrap metal? Companies emerging from bankruptcy?), you can almost certainly find a related investment product.

Moreover, these new products—particularly the emergence of exchange-traded funds (or ETFs)—have made investing in once-inaccessible markets deceptively easy, particularly for the smaller investor. A decade or so ago, getting access to overseas stock funds might have required tens of thousands of dollars as a minimum investment. You would also have had to pay high management fees and operating costs. Now, global investing looks easy; just $1,000 or so in an emerging markets ETF and you've got exposure to the potential profits you believe it offers. Of course, the risks may be equally outsized, a fact that the ease of access overshadows. In 1994, investors in fledgling Latin American markets lost big; those who made hefty profits on emerging Asian economies in countries like Korea and Thailand did the same in 1997 and 1998. That rout sent emerging market indexes down as much as 40% during the 12-month period that ended in July 1998. More recently, investors in Chinese stocks have experienced equally outsize losses.

So, what's a beleaguered investor to do? It's a bit like walking into the world's largest supermarket without a shopping list or meal plan in your hands. In the financial supermarket, there are thousands of different investments you can make, in dozens of different countries, and as well as at least a dozen asset classes. Meanwhile, pundits tell you repeatedly to "buy what you know" and assure you that solid research and hard work will give you an edge. The temptation to believe that it's just a matter of putting a few important analytical tools to work is irresistible; with those, the task of investment picking will become simple and straightforward. That conviction isn't confined to the ranks of the ordinary retail investor, those who flock to events like the Money Show hoping to learn more about price/earnings ratios and other stock-picking tools. At the other end of the spectrum, every summer, tens of thousands of business school graduates take to the streets of New York, Boston, San Francisco, and Chicago. Armed with their cutting-edge HP 12-C financial calculators, which can compute an internal rate of return with the touch of a button, and an air of invincibility, they sally forth. These fledgling investment research analysts are under orders from their employers—perhaps Fidelity Investments, perhaps the newest hedge fund on the block—to seek out the best stock investment ideas in the industry they have been assigned to cover. Needless to say, quality research is critical, especially if you rely on it to help you select securities.

What's interesting is that even as experienced market veterans and green retail investors continue to scour the landscape in search of their ideal—a pharmaceutical company that has suddenly broken through scientific roadblocks to devise a cure for cancer, say, or a technology company that has developed a new gizmo that consumers will never want to live without and that competitors can never match—a new theory of investing has been taking hold. Professor Burton Malkiel pioneered what is now called the efficient market hypothesis; the best summary is still found in his groundbreaking book *A Random Walk Down Wall Street: The Time-Tested Strategy for Successful Investing.* (First published in 1973, the bestseller has never been out of print.) The essence of this theory is that at any given point of time, the prices of all stocks and bonds in any market accurately reflect whatever news and analysis exists. News is unpredictable, and it is impossible to say how any given stock, bond, currency, or commodity will react to a particular piece of economic data or political catastrophe. This extreme theory suggests discarding the fundamental analysis that many professional money managers swear by, or technical analysis, in which investors try to get an edge on the market by scrutinizing historical price patterns of various securities or markets. The only way for investors to win, according to Malkiel's thesis, is to put all their assets into a basket of securities that accurately reflects the market (an index fund) and stay put for the long haul.

Malkiel makes an interesting case. In a recent follow-up study, he reported his discovery that over periods of 10 years or more, some 80% of stock funds run by "active" managers (those who pick individual securities they believed would outperform) ended up with *lower* returns than stock market benchmarks or passively managed funds tied to individual indexes. The same pattern held true in international investing, where active money managers often claim stock picking is vital because markets are less efficient. Standard & Poor's demonstrated this in a study of investment returns over a 5-year period ending in December 2006, in which analysts studied the ability of mutual fund managers to end up in the top half of their peer group in each of those years. As it turned out, only 13.2% of large-cap fund managers did so in each of the five 12-month periods. It was just as hard for a fund to follow one good year with another one: Only 17.3% of large-cap funds that posted top-quartile returns in the 5 years ended December 2001 managed to repeat that performance in the following 5-year period.[1] Not surprisingly, Malkiel sticks to his conclusion that investors fare better when they invest in low-cost index funds rather than investment products run by active stock pickers.

But Malkiel's hypothesis doesn't cover the vagaries of human behavior. Sure, over the long haul, rationality rules. But in the short term, as academics like Yale University's Robert Schiller have argued, fear, greed, and other investor sentiments tend to drive stock markets to often-absurd extremes. One example that has become almost a cliché of how rational investment decisions morph into an irrational mania, is the seventeenth-century Dutch tulip-bulb craze. When Carolus Clusius brought a fascinating collection of new plants from Turkey when he arrived to take up his position as a botany professor at the university in Leyden in 1593, he couldn't have expected the insanity that would follow. Tulips quickly became a staple in the gardens of prosperous Dutch burghers. Then, a few decades later, a virus caused a mutation in the flowers, producing an array of stripes or "flames" in contrasting colors that hypnotized the Dutch and made the new bulbs too valuable to be left in flowerbeds. An entire industry grew up around the new hybrid bulbs, with specialist merchants trying to predict—and stockpile—the most popular color combinations. Tulip mania was born. Speculators traded options on future tulip bulbs, and by January 1637, bulb prices soared twentyfold in a single month. Hordes of irrational investors were willing to swap real estate and jewelry for the most coveted bulbs. The next month, bulb prices collapsed, taking the Dutch economy with them.

Malkiel's theories overlook a powerful element of human nature: the inability of most people to resist the allure of whatever "investment" has been most successful recently. (That's exactly why regulators require mutual fund companies to spell out in any ad for their products that past performance is no guarantee of what will happen in the future.) Indeed, the bigger the recent gain, the more willing investors seem to be to toss caution to the wind. Ultimately, they become so caught up in their pursuit of riches that they can't distinguish between a legitimate (if overpriced) investment opportunity and an illicit pyramid scheme.

Paradoxically, it's easy to prove that winning streaks aren't always sustainable. At Harris Private Bank, my team recently reviewed returns on large-cap stocks, long-term government and corporate bonds, and intermediate notes and Treasury bills over a 78-year period beginning in 1926 and ending in 2004. During that time frame, stocks returned an annualized 10.3%, with a standard deviation of 20.3%. (A standard deviation measures the degree of variation from the expected return, and serves as a way of expressing risk levels numerically; the higher the standard deviation, the greater the risk and the possibility of losing your investment.) A quick way to "guesstimate" the range of annual returns possible or likely given a set of return and standard deviation figures is to add 20.3%, the standard deviation, to 10.3%, the expected return to determine an upside return, then subtract 20.3% from 10.3% to determine an "expected" downside. That means the maximum possible return someone could realistically expect roughly two-thirds of the time is 30.6% (the first figure), while taking that level of risk created the possibility of a 10% loss (the second figure). Along with my analysts, I tried to determine what would have happened each year if we had constructed a portfolio built entirely of the preceding year's top performer. The result? Annualized returns were only marginally higher than the index delivered—10.6% compared to 10.3%—but the standard deviation was significantly higher at 21.6%, meaning that an investor chasing top performers would have taken on more risk and experienced more volatility. (Losses could have hit 11%.) The best option proved to be a balanced portfolio, one with 60% invested in large-cap stocks, 30% in small-cap stocks, 5% in long-term corporate bonds and 5% in Treasury bills and that was rebalanced annually to maintain that weighting. That generated higher absolute returns—an annualized 11%—and had a lower standard deviation than the portfolio composed only of "winners."

Recent history serves to remind us that human nature may be the biggest obstacle to structuring a diversified portfolio that stands a better chance of performing over the long haul. At the height of the dot. com boom, I was running a wealth management firm in Ponte Vedra Beach, Florida, managing portfolios of $3 million or more for wealthy individuals and their families. It was frustrating. My goal was to manage my clients' wealth for the long haul. But every time I met with a client or even attended a dinner party, people demanded my opinion on the latest Internet innovation or a tip on the best way to play the need for greater bandwidth. Most difficult of all were the meetings with prospective clients. These folks were intelligent enough to have amassed in their own business or profession what by most standards would be considered a fortune. Now they allegedly were seeking someone to protect and manage that capital. But did they *really* want my expertise? Even as I presented my qualifications, reviewed my capabilities, and explained the services I could offer, I was aware that over the past year or two many of my potential clients had handily outperformed my carefully constructed model portfolios thanks to one or two lucky bets on technology stocks like Veritas or Broadcom. Why, these folks clearly wondered, should they hire me when it was obvious that I couldn't do better for them than they were already doing?

But when individual investors believe it's easy to build a top-performing portfolio using a few individual stock picks, it's time to head for the hills. Indeed, within 2 years, the dot.com bubble had exploded, leaving a trail of wreckage in its place. Those of us who valued process over pizzazz suddenly looked wise again; the speculators lived to regret their foolhardiness in betting their wealth on stocks such as Pets.com. Many will never see their portfolios recover, and some retirees were even forced back into the workplace to compensate for their losses. Building a portfolio is *not* easy; it requires sorting through a mountain of data and a vast array of investment options. It also means being especially alert when markets are irrational.

Just how hard is it to evaluate a single stock? A dedicated stock picker will tell you it's easy—just study the company's annual report or financial statements and look at its price and financial ratios. But many of the factors that dictate a company's share price never show up in these documents, as I came to realize. That's why most of us rely on professional research analysts to evaluate individual issues. Back in 1997, when Pepsico spun off its fast-food chain operator, Tricon Global (later to be renamed Yum Brands), as an independent, publicly traded company, I decided that the cash flow they generated selling pepperoni pizzas and buckets full of extra-crispy chicken at food courts nationwide was attractive enough to snap up some shares in the aftermath of the initial public offering. After all, I rationalized, if there's one thing I can count on, it's that the American consumer's passion for tasty high-fat treats will triumph over likely future heart-burn any day of the week. And with brands like KFC, Pizza Hut, and Taco Bell under their roof, Yum Brands was well positioned to keep benefiting from that trend. Of course, I scrutinized the company's public reports and other publicly available information, looking for anything that would signal a flaw in my logic. It turned out that a crucial piece of information—that some genetically modified corn, not approved for human consumption, had snuck its way into the production line of Taco Bell brand tortilla chips—was nowhere to be found until it was reported in the media in July 2000. The reason? The chips weren't made by Yum Brands and were sold in grocery stores rather than the fast-food outlets. But all that mattered was the brand association. Shares of Yum Brands plunged 24% within 3 weeks, erasing every penny of the profit I had made since the initial public stock offering 3 years earlier.

Any time an investor buys an individual stock, he or she could be signing up for a rollercoaster ride of this kind. So Malkiel's thinking needs to be combined with other analytical tools, especially given the fact that entire markets or asset classes can be pricey or cheap on both an absolute and relative basis at different points in time and generate wildly divergent returns over the course of any given year. All of us have seen, for instance, how between 2004 and 2007, stock markets struggled to eke out modest single-digit returns as commodity investment funds soared. In that kind of investment environment, advising someone to go for a random walk or only focus on pure valuation levels of individual companies isn't good enough. What is needed is an investment approach that understands valuations for market indexes, each of which contain hundreds or sometimes even thousands of different stocks, bonds, or other securities. This kind of big-picture approach, or "macro" investment strategy, is at once more inviting and more statistically robust for investors trying to capture some incremental returns.

So, what's the secret sauce—the vital ingredient for an investor who wants to maximize his or her returns? Macro investing is all about finding a way to evaluate markets, rather than focusing just on individual stocks. Investors have limited time at their disposal, even as the array of investment options that they are asked to pass judgment on continues to expand rapidly. Whenever someone makes an investment decision, consciously or unconsciously they are working through a series of decisions like the one in Figure 2.1, what I refer to as a decision matrix.

At each level of this matrix, decisions have a certain payoff or return. The more specific the decision, the lower the likely payoff. Let's say that you're trying to decide whether to invest in large- or small-cap stocks, and are thinking of adding an extra 10% of your

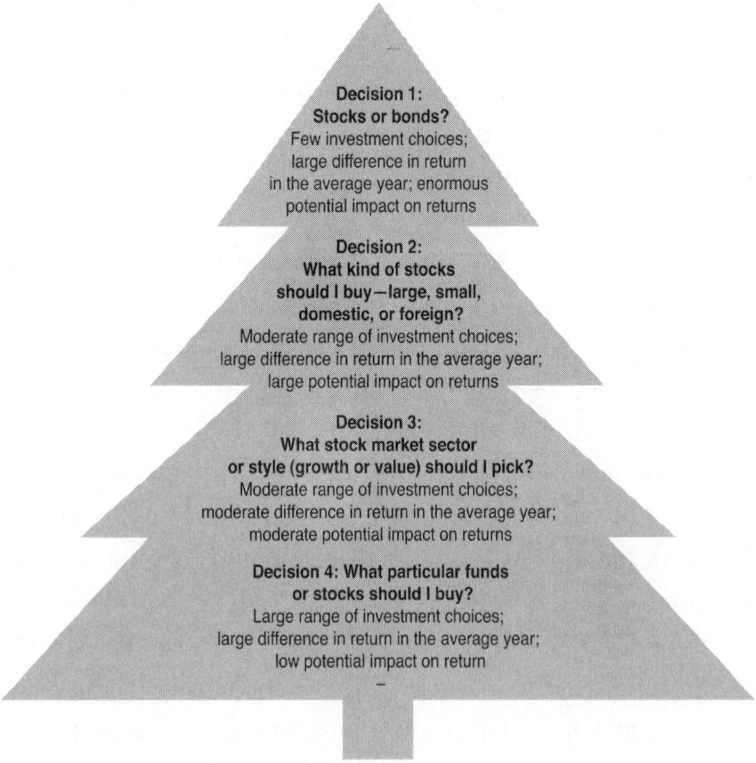

Decision 1:
Stocks or bonds?
Few investment choices;
large difference in return
in the average year; enormous
potential impact on returns

Decision 2:
What kind of stocks
should I buy—large, small,
domestic, or foreign?
Moderate range of investment choices;
large difference in return in the average year;
large potential impact on returns

Decision 3:
What stock market sector
or style (growth or value) should I pick?
Moderate range of investment choices;
moderate difference in return in the average year;
moderate potential impact on returns

Decision 4: What particular funds
or stocks should I buy?
Large range of investment choices;
large difference in return in the average year;
low potential impact on return
–

Figure 2.1   The decision tree.

portfolio to whichever you decide. Given that the average difference of the return on the Standard & Poor's 500 Index (the large-stock benchmark) and the Russell 2000 Index (the small-cap bellwether) hovers around 10 percentage points at any given point in time, this gives you the chance to boost your returns by a full percentage point—from 8% a year to 9%, say. Over the years, given the magic of compound returns, that translates into enough extra money to spell the difference between retiring early in your 50s to your dream home and still working in your 70s to make ends meet. The more diligently you study these macro-level valuation discrepancies, the more accurately you will be able to predict the times when you need to make asset-allocation shifts. (At times, the performance gap between the two benchmarks has reached an astonishing 30 percentage points!) The harsh reality is that not only do more macro-level decisions further up that "decision tree" take less time to make, but they also offer you the biggest potential returns with the least risk. Face it: If you were in the middle of a minefield, wouldn't you get out of it more rapidly and with greater confidence if you knew there were only 3 mines in a 3-acre area, instead of 300?

Macro-level investing means investors focusing on industry groups, sectors, or asset classes. Take a look at the medical devices arena—a compelling but ultra-volatile part of the healthcare industry. Here, picking the "winner" can spell the difference between success and failure, as is obvious by the jostling for position in just one area, the field of pacemakers and coronary stents. Medtronic and St. Jude Medical wage a fierce battle for preeminence, and investment analysts track their successes and failures on a quarterly basis and scramble to predict which has the edge at any given second. It's downright exhausting—but seems crucial, because although Medtronic's stock rose twice as much as that of St. Jude between 1997 and 2001, their fortunes reversed. Over the next 5 years, St. Jude outperformed Medtronic by a whopping 400%. But just a minute. Why should you, the investor, back one of these two companies at the expense of the other, just because they choose to compete so ferociously?

In fact, the simplest and lowest-risk solution in that 10-year period would have been to buy and hold stock in *both* companies. Medtronic delivered an annualized return of 12.5% and St. Jude an annualized 16% over the course of that decade, with standard deviations of 29.7% and 36.9%, respectively. So, for each "unit" of risk taken, Medtronic returned 0.42%, while St. Jude delivered 0.44%. An investor deciding to invest equally in both competitors would have captured an annualized 14.4% return, with a 26.8% standard deviation, meaning he would have taken less risk than he would have by betting on just one of the two rivals. Even better, he would have eliminated the biggest part of his research headache—the need to keep track of the perpetual battle between the two rivals and to guess the point at which one will take over the lead. Add in a third player, Boston Scientific, and the risk-return scenario becomes still more attractive; an equal-weighted portfolio generated 0.54% of return for each "unit" of risk taken. The result? An annualized return and risk level that are both better than two out of the three stocks (see Table 2.1).

What is true of industry sectors applies all the way up the decision tree. Any time that an investor can make fewer decisions

TABLE 2.1 Building a Risk-Adjusted Healthcare Portfolio. Source: Bloomberg

	Annual Return	Standard Deviation	Return Versus Risk
Boston Scientific	1.2%	8.2%	0.15
Medtronic	12.5%	29.7%	0.42
St. Jude	16.0%	36.9%	0.44
Equally Weighted Portfolio	14.4%	26.8%	0.54

10-year Performance through December 2007

at the upper levels of that tree, the odds improve that he or she can do so with the help of more and more reliable information. So, too, do the odds that these decisions will help to boost investment returns and curb risk levels. The term for this approach, *global macro,* sounds fancy enough to require a small fleet of Gulfstream IV jets and offices in 37 countries. But all it means in practice is taking this kind of approach to every sector and market in which you invest. Rather than analyze each stock or bond in isolation, this macro approach places nearly all markets on a level playing field. Are foreign stocks more attractive than their domestic counterparts, or is the battered real estate market a better option than either?

The goal is twofold. First, global macro investing simplifies the investment process because it means you don't have to spend time following every little hiccup in the performance of a few hundred stocks in your portfolio and outside it. At the same time, you can inject more certainty into the decision-making process. In essence, by pushing up the decision-making tree to the topmost levels, global macro strategies permit you to minimize your exposure to risky and overvalued segments and increase your allocation to those asset classes that offer the most compelling risk/reward tradeoff.

It all boils down to active asset allocation: the ability to identify when it is time to increase your exposure to stocks, bonds, commodities, or real estate. The key to success is devising an investment process that regularly evaluates markets in an attempt to identify areas that are overpriced and risky as well as those that contain hidden value. Over an adequate time horizon (let's say 1 to 3 years), a global macro investor can use this process to add significant incremental return. In contrast, between markets or asset classes it is not only easier to predict the range of returns you can capture but also where you are likely to get the biggest bang for your buck. That's because the best-performing market can outperform the worst by as much as 70 percentage points in any given year. If you make your investment decisions at the asset-allocation level, you almost immediately boost the odds that your portfolio will outperform the market. That's because asset classes, as a rule, contain fewer surprises than individual stocks—just ask thousands of Lehman Brothers stockholders left lamenting the evaporation of their investment in the firm! Of course, they would have suffered losses in the broader financial sector in those turbulent months in the autumn of 2008, but would have fared better had they diversified across a sector or, better yet, the asset class of stocks as a whole. And because asset classes are less volatile than individual stocks, it is not only simpler but for smaller investors, less expensive to construct a portfolio: Sometimes as few as five or six holdings can offer enough diversification, thanks to the magic of ETFs.

The key to detecting market mispricings of asset classes and industry sectors is data—the right data, used the right way. My own conviction that being able to measure market dynamics would help me become a better investor dates back to a brief conversation with then-CIA director Robert Gates in 1991. At the time, I was working in Boston for Eagle Investment Associates, a division of Bank of Boston. Some of the world's most sophisticated investment professionals, such as Fidelity Investments's guru, Peter Lynch, were trustees for entities that had entrusted their assets to us. It was downright intimidating to have to stand up in front of experts like Lynch and bring them up-to-date on how their portfolios had fared under my management.

My epiphany occurred in the boardroom of Draper Laboratories, an extremely low-profile joint venture between the Massachusetts Institute of Technology and the U.S. military, for whom I managed part of their endowment. In that pre-9/11 era, the security seemed enormous; before I could talk to the trustees about what the markets were doing, I had to pass a background check. After that kind of introduction, the rather austere meeting room, furnished with Formica tables and metal chairs, seemed a bit anticlimactic. My self-confidence returned as I presented my investment outlook. I was rather bullish; the economy was emerging from a recession, and the yield curve suggested that economic growth would accelerate. I noted that the price/earnings ratio on stocks was low—another bullish signal, as was the fact that credit spreads (the extra interest income lenders demand in return for loans) were tightening. That was a hint that lenders were becoming more optimistic. After my upbeat presentation, I asked whether anyone had questions. A pause; then a hand went up. It belonged to a rather laconic but self-confident board member, who introduced himself as Robert Gates. He wasn't an investment person, he admitted, but he asked whether the data I had just presented as a reason for my bullish outlook was data that I had selected because it supported my theory. Or was it data that I consistently tracked, hoping to detect signs of change? Sheepishly, I had to respond that it, in this case, was more the former than the latter.

Gates might not have known much about investing, but whenever the director of the Central Intelligence Agency talks about how to use and interpret data, you listen. He suggested that if I could identify a set of data that, over a period of time, provided reliable information about the market and the economy, then I could track that data over time to pick up subtle shifts. Those incremental changes could, in turn, shape and modify my investment outlook and provide me with an edge in detecting inflection points in a wide array of asset classes. Initially, I saw his suggestion as a professional challenge. Thinking it through, however, I realized that finding a way to measure market dynamics would be vital to my long-term success as an investor and money manager.

It took me years to develop such a process, and I continue to refine and adapt it today, but it has already proven its value. Beginning with the recognition that human weaknesses play a great role in our investment decisions, this "global macro" and inductive decision-making process is one that I am convinced spells the difference between building a modest retirement nest egg and turning those savings into a level of affluence that spells true wealth. And the first step to build that decision-making process is understanding the need to insulate yourself from the human flaw that is most dangerous of all to any investor: You must find a way to be sure that you don't let emotions like greed and fear replace cold, hard logic in that investment model.

Endnotes

[1] Burton Malkiel, *A Random Walk Down Wall Street: The Time Tested Strategy for Successful Investing* (New York: W.W. Norton & Company, 1973).

3

Exploit Your Edge; Eliminate Your Weakness I—Beating the Street

Developing an investment process is not for the faint of heart. You have to be ruthless and level-headed when it comes to evaluating not just your portfolio but yourself and your own emotions. The first step toward surviving the jungle of the financial markets is to take a long hard look at yourself. Only then will you recognize the ways your own instincts—everything from your eagerness to believe that hard work is enough to basic human emotions such as greed, fear, pride, and an addiction to excitement—can undermine your ability to remain calm in the face of a noisy and chaotic market. Only then can you realistically evaluate your own abilities and limitations and learn to discern when and where you really possess an "edge" in the market.

Skeptical? Just think about the market meltdown of 2008, when emotions ran amok. Of course, there were plenty of cogent reasons for selling stocks that autumn. The credit markets were caught in a deep freeze, leaving otherwise sound companies without access to short-term capital to finance their operating costs. In the wake of the collapse of two investment banks and the overnight sale of Merrill Lynch & Co. to Bank of America, not even the savviest or most venerable investor could predict what might happen next, and risk aversion soared to unprecedented levels. That sent the stock market into a tailspin. Clearly, some of those sellers *had* to sell to meet margin calls or raise capital to stay in business. But along with this kind of "rational" selling came a kind of indiscriminate downward pressure that I can only call *spectator selling:* Panicking, individuals dumped everything they owned onto the market in hope of finding a buyer at any price. Emotions took over.

Whenever individual investors begin to chase the market, they lose. That will prove to be the case with the market meltdown of 2008, as many investors almost certainly will end up repurchasing securities they dumped at rock-bottom prices during the midst of the panic at much higher valuations once enough time has passed that we can all separate the truly troubled companies from those that happened to be in the wrong place at the wrong time (that is, traded on any global stock exchange in the second half of 2008). As individuals, what we imagine to be our "edge"—our conviction that we have a knack for picking stocks on our own that will outperform the market—is in fact a weakness. Even after 25 years in the trenches, I still get tempted by an exciting story about an individual stock. Hot stocks are dramatic. When you win with one, it's as if you had won the lottery, but even better because you can lay claim to insight and judgment rather than just dumb luck. But hot stocks are elusive, and their pursuit is much more likely to cost you money than earn you rich returns.

Your edge lies, ironically, in your willingness to acknowledge that as an individual investor you're at a big disadvantage when it comes to unearthing not only the stock market's buried gems but even the most straightforward and solid investment strategy. For individual investors, picking stocks is an uphill battle. Even the pros can have challenges. For example, Bill Miller, managing the Legg Mason Value Trust since 1992, beat the S&P 500 for 15 years running before failing to do so again in 2006. (Miller's closest rivals in 2006, each with a 7-year winning streak, were two obscure funds with offbeat and risky investment strategies.) Firms like Legg Mason continue devoting millions of dollars in resources each year to trying to beat a market index, and they have the ability to do that. Boston-based Fidelity Investments, for instance, now handles $1 trillion in assets, and can well afford to pay six-digit salaries to each of their 180 or so in-house research analysts in the hope that each of them will find at least one brilliant idea amid the thousands of global businesses whose financial statements and filings they peruse 60 hours or more each week. Across the industry as a whole, there are now about 91,000 money managers and investment analysts who have survived many years of study and three rigorous examinations to win the title of Chartered Financial Analyst. Thousands more are working toward that certification, or working without it. Many are being well paid to do nothing but work away to find the next stock market winner.

When you decide to build an investment process as an individual investor that revolves around stock picking, you're going up against all those bright minds and all those resources. That's why investors value quality research. You may yearn to find the brilliant idea that somehow escapes this vast net cast by the investment industry; the odds, however, say that you won't. Yes, in the Internet era, any investor has access to most of the documents and reports they need to identify a company that is struggling under too much debt or one whose new product is poised to become a bestseller. The goal of Regulation FD, a rule imposed by the Securities & Exchange Commission that requires a company to disclose material facts, was to remove institutional advantages that the pros possess. No longer can the CEO of a manufacturing company legally provide extra insight into a new contract to institutional money managers without providing that disclosure at the same time to the rest of the world. But there are some built-in advantages that no regulatory edict can remove. For instance, you're not going to quit your day job to study financial statements in hopes of passing the CFA examinations, are you? Just as an investment analyst can't repair a heart valve, a cardiac surgeon doesn't have the specialized knowledge that the pros accumulate doing their job one day after the next, year after year.

Just how large is the advantage that the pros enjoy when it comes to picking stocks? Well, they have Bloomberg terminals sitting on their desks that, at a cost of anywhere from $17,000 to $21,000 a year, deliver everything from the basic stock quotes to news and complex analytical models. They are great, and I admit my job would be much more difficult without one on my desk. But let's face it, if you're trying to build wealth, spending this much annually isn't the most rational thing you can do. And you need more than the Bloomberg: Your shopping list should include an annual subscription to *Baseline* or *Factset* to obtain other critical data (another $12,000 a year) and independent investment research from at least two different firms (about $20,000 each). So before you have made a single investment decision, you have accumulated perhaps $70,000 in annual expenses, all of which will need to be recouped through the investment ideas that they generate. And I haven't even mentioned the cost of subscribing to a real-time data service or the expenses of going to industry conferences in person to get access to the same insights the Fidelity team can obtain with a phone call. Daunted yet? Then let's also factor in the cost of human capital—all those skilled traders that firms like Fidelity hire to be sure the "buy" and "sell" ideas are executed at just the right price, or the technology geeks who makes sure your computer runs properly. Hedge funds go still further, hiring industry experts to offer their insights into whatever industry is attracting the fund manager's attention in the same way a lawyer might hire an expert witness to defend a murderer on trial.

To you or me—as individuals—the financial cost of becoming a well-informed stock picker is prohibitively high. To the average institution, however, it's far easier—the price of entry into the business. And there are more intangible benefits that come from being part of an organization devoted to hunting for great investment ideas. For instance, an investor working for Goldman Sachs can pick up the phone at any time of the day to talk to traders in Hong Kong or London about what is happening to a stock there, or to obtain insight from a local analyst about the potential demand for iPods in the Chinese market. Sometimes it's that extra smidgen of data or piece of insight that leads to the best investment ideas—and individual investors don't have easy access to that network.

Being part of that network brings other benefits. Insider trading may be illegal (although it certainly still takes place), but not all cases of privileged access to corporate information come under the heading of insider trading. If you happen to meet a CEO of a company and have extensive discussions with him or her, one on one, you may well decide that this is a particularly canny individual who will transform the company into a top performer. If you aren't a member of the investment world, or part of that CEO's personal network, however, what are the odds that you'll be able to have that chat in the first place? Remember that although investors in Internet and Biotech IPO shares at the time of their initial public offering fared very well indeed, the serious money was generally made by those company's earliest backers. These include venture capitalists, but also other members of their extended circles, all of whom invested privately in the company while it was still a tiny start-up. Investors in many of those IPOs fared pretty well. However, the original insiders generally fared much better.

Then there are the junkets, the trips organized by companies for professional investors, in hopes of persuading them to buy shares. I don't often venture out on this kind of expedition, but I was curious enough about the Canadian oil sands—described by *Time* magazine as "Canada's greatest buried energy treasure," oil reserves that may be second only to those of Saudi Arabia and which some argue may be able to meet the world's insatiable hunger for petroleum products for the remainder of the twenty-first century— to venture to northern Alberta on a trip organized by Shell Canada. Along with two dozen analysts and portfolio managers, I hopped aboard an elderly retired turbo-prop commuter plane in Calgary for the hour-long flight to North America's latest boomtown, Fort McMurray. Rattling along its bumpy and still unpaved roads in the yellow school bus sent to the airstrip's Quonset hut to transport us to Shell Canada's Albian Sands operation, we felt woefully out of place in our sports jackets and neatly pressed khaki pants as we drove past hastily constructed concrete block apartment buildings and bars. The trip accomplished what it was supposed to, however: Without exception, our jaws dropped in awe at the scale of the operation. Enormous dump-truck-like vehicles, with tires measuring a whopping 12 feet in diameter, transport massive amounts of sand excavated from the ground to the silos where the process of stripping the increasingly valuable "heavy oil" from the sand itself begins, with two tons of oily sand required to produce a single barrel of oil.

Investment analysts exist to help the rest of the market sort through the universe of investment opportunities and help us understand whether or not an oil sands 'play' is, indeed, a good addition to a portfolio. But even if you and I had access to all the research reports cranked out each year, would we end up making better investment decisions? Not necessarily. Even if we could winnow our way through the forest and focus on one or two trees, the odds are still that we, as individual investors, would be late to the party. Another edge for the pros is their ability to build a diversified portfolio rapidly; your ability to match them or beat them is remote. Individuals who have recognized their disadvantage have hired financial advisors to invest on their behalf.

Let's say that every time you visit Bed Bath & Beyond to replace your vacuum cleaner, or to buy a new coffee grinder or bath towels, you have been impressed how many fellow shoppers are making big purchases. The company's financial statements confirm that your firsthand impressions were on the money. And—the last item on your checklist—the analyst reports you have read from Smith Barney and ValueLine all say the stock is screaming "buy" at its current valuations. Whoa! Stop, take a deep breath. Remember that Bed Bath & Beyond's stock *already* reflects the collective decisions of many of those professional analysts and investment managers. When it comes

savvy investors might miss. The trick on how to profit from this expertise is to combine active stock picking in the sector where you *do* have an edge with more passive investing in other market sectors, from technology to health care to retailing. Go ahead, overweight Chubb—just don't succumb to the temptation to think that makes you an expert about Bed Bath & Beyond's prospects.

There are two ways to exploit this particular edge. Both require you to be able to compile a list of stocks in your industry that you expect to be winners, along with another that you believe will be laggards. The purest way for a retired insurance executive to transform his or her knowledge into stock-market-beating profits is to buy the "forecast winners" stocks while simultaneously selling short the "forecast losers." (Short selling means borrowing the stock and selling it in the expectation of being able to repurchase and replace that borrowed stock at a lower price later on, the profit being the difference between the two prices. It's a risky strategy, because the loss can theoretically be infinite.) As long as you get it right (and don't underestimate how difficult that is) and the returns from your expected winners materialize while your forecast losers stumble, you should be able to book profits on your portfolio regardless of what the rest of the market is doing. In a bull market environment, if the winners return an average of 15% and the "losers" manage to eke out a 5% return, you may end up losing money on your short positions, but you're still ahead 10%. In a bear market, as long as the losers decline by more than the "forecast winners" do, you'll still emerge with a net profit on these positions. To ensure that you outpace the S&P 500, all you need to do is take that net profit from those trades and invest it in an S&P 500 futures contract, which promises its owner the return on that index as well as any appreciation in the value of the futures contract itself.

An alternative strategy for investors who aren't comfortable with the degree of risk involved in selling short is to take an index-like position in all the stocks and sectors in the S&P 500, identical in weighting to those in the index—with the exception of the insurance industry. You then take the 4.3% index exposure to insurance in the

S&P 500 and invest that money actively, picking only those stocks that you believe will outperform and overweighting them. Again, as long as you get the winners right, you'll beat the S&P.

The biggest problem with this strategy is that investors usually don't have that level of expertise or insight into any given industry. Three decades as a successful cardiac surgeon might give anyone insight into how well certain medical devices perform in practice, but not into the many other factors that determine what makes one next-generation cardiac monitoring system a success and another a failure. Most investors who opt to use stock picking as the basis of their investment process will, at some point, have to rely on investment research to help build a diversified portfolio. Much of this is generated by the same folks I mentioned earlier, those devoted full time to their analytical work and with access to all the resources a big investment firm can offer. Why not tap into their collective wisdom? If you can't beat them, why not join them, by signing on the dotted line and becoming a client of one (say, Morgan Stanley)?

The research community has had its share of challenges, although most of them have been removed in recent years after the scandal in which Citigroup's star telecommunications analyst, Jack Grubman, was shown to have compromised his objectivity. In what proved to be just the most blatant of many such deals across Wall Street, Grubman agreed to put a buy rating on AT&T stock—a rating his CEO, Sandy Weill, wanted to have to win underwriting business from AT&T—in exchange for a big donation by Weill to a Manhattan preschool in which Grubman was trying to enroll his twin toddlers. Ultimately, in April 2003, ten of the largest Wall Street firms agreed to pay $1.4 billion in fines for having published biased research, as part of a pact settling pending regulatory investigations by the Securities and Exchange Commission.

In addition to using quality research, what about entrusting your money to a successful money manager, and count on him or her to pick the right stocks? At any given time, there are plenty of successful money managers in the market. There also, however, "hot hands" in the market: money managers who achieve eye-popping investment returns during a period in which their area of expertise and talents coincide exactly with what is required to identify that handful of stocks that the market will reward in the coming year or so. But inevitably, their moment in the sun will pass. Think of all the Internet and dot.com stock pickers lauded in the pages of the financial press in 1999. Where are they now? Alberto Vilar ran afoul of regulators and wound up convicted of fraud for looting his clients' accounts to finance his philanthropic donations after the dot.com bubble burst in 2000 and left him strapped for cash. In 1998, Ryan Jacob, then 29 years old, posted returns of 196% and opened his own Internet fund the following year. The new fund quickly lost 95% of its assets as the dot.com bubble burst, and Jacob has battled to boost its size back above $100 million—well below the $500 million plus he had to play with at its peak.

No one has managed to demonstrate scientifically what skills are required to outperform the market, but Thomas McGuigan, president of Beyond Tomorrow Strategic Advisors LLC in Guilford, Connecticut, has proven how difficult it is to accomplish that feat. In a 2006 study, he and his team took the performance of all mutual funds investing in large-capitalization U.S. stocks over the 20-year period ending November 30, 2003. A mere 10.59% of those funds beat the S&P 500 in that time period, but over rolling 10-year periods, 24.71% of the funds outperformed the index. Intrigued, McGuigan delved more deeply into the results. The result? For every manager who could claim to have outperformed the index, more than one lagged; while 2 funds outperformed the S&P 500 over the 20-year study period by between 1 and 2 percentage points, 37 trailed by the same amount. McGuigan's next question was whether historic performance said anything about a fund manager's ability to outperform in the future. Alas, managers who outperformed in the first decade lagged in the second 10-year period. Only 28.5% of top-quintile performers hung on to their position in that elite group in the second decade, regardless of whether they were investing in large- or small-cap stocks.

So what is an investor's edge in this kind of Darwinian struggle? A significant part of it lies in the investor acknowledging that he or she is at a disadvantage when it comes to trying to pick the best-performing stocks. Why compete with the professional investors head to head on what remains anything but a level playing field? As an independent investor, your "added edge" can be your ability to pick markets. "Are stocks the right asset class to be in at this time?" is one key question to ask, not "what stock is going to make my fortune?" Instead of only asking which technology fund manager has the top track record, the better strategy is to also look at the bigger picture. "Are small stocks or large-cap stocks more attractive in this environment?"

These questions are ones you are more likely to be able to answer and are more likely to lead to sensible investment decisions. Paradoxically, they are also the questions too often ignored or overlooked by inferior money managers who struggle to generate sustained periods of outperformance. You as an individual investor have the relative luxury of being able to put your investment capital wherever you want—wherever the returns seem most appealing or the risk seems to be lowest. That is part of your edge, made even more compelling by the fact that often the well-paid teams of professionals don't have the same flexibility. Pension funds and other institutions that choose professionals to manage their assets don't typically favor picking those who adopt a global macro approach. Most asset-allocation decisions have already been made by the investment consultants that pension fund and endowment trustees retain. The consultant who wins a mandate to advise a pension fund, college endowment, or other big pool of capital starts off by analyzing the risk profile and liquidity needs of that fund, based on a survey of its assets and obligations, and then prescribes a target allocation to various markets (stocks, bonds, real estate, commodities, hedge funds, and so on) that matches those liquidity needs and the fund's overall risk profile. For each designated market, the consultant goes on to pick, from a short list, the manager it believes will do best at delivering a portfolio that will fare better than its peers. Let's say that both you and that consultant invest in the same small-cap stock fund. You have different goals in mind. The consultant wants the fund to beat its index and its peers, you want it to make money. The two don't always go hand in hand. Small-cap stocks can be out of favor, and if you've backed a relative outperformer, you're still going to be losing money, while the consultant is reconciled to that, because his client's needs are different.

Traditionally, consultants' methodology shuns tactical asset allocation; the process of rebalancing assets on an ongoing basis in response to what is happening within the financial markets, reacting to new opportunities and the emergence of new risks. That is just what you, as an individual investor, need: an investment process that depends on a rigorous and constantly updated analysis of what is happening within the stock or bond market. A large-cap money manager is going to have large-cap stocks—with their distinctive characteristics—in his or her portfolio at all times, regardless of how attractive they are relative to small-cap stocks or emerging markets bonds. That manager doesn't have a choice, but you do. And that is your edge.

So why do so many investors continue to overlook their edge and instead emphasize their weakness by competing with the resource-heavy pros to try to select only individual stocks? Tens of thousands of individuals subscribe to stock-picking newsletters; hundreds of thousands to monthly magazines that each and every month promise to give them the names of, say, the top seven recession-proof stocks or the best "green" energy stock plays. And millions still tune in daily to Jim Cramer's show on CNBC. The harsh truth? Even once we acknowledge the many institutional challenges of stock picking, before we can add a more rational global macro investment process we still must be prepared to battle another of our biggest weaknesses: human nature.

4

Exploit Your Edge; Eliminate Your Weakness II—Battling Yourself

I am my own worst enemy—but at least I know it. After 25 years in the investment world, I have gradually learned to notice the warning signs that try to alert me to an attempted takeover by my instincts. Most of the time, I am able to ensure that my hard-won professional judgment triumphs in these battles, which is why I can say that my mantra, shared with many other investment advisers, is that "my clients pay me to lose sleep at night so that they don't have to." And I do lose sleep, because navigating the financial markets is never simple or straightforward. Like many of you, I endure market plunges with about the same level of fortitude as I cope with severe turbulence on an airplane flight: I tighten my seatbelt while wishing I could parachute to safety. "Why didn't I sell?" I'll ask myself, almost angrily. But I can just as easily get caught up in the euphoria of a bull market, merrily following a trend line to the sky.

You may not need to stretch out on an analyst's couch for an intensive round of therapy before embarking on an investment program, but it might not hurt. The truth is that our own personalities and our opinions of the way the world *should* work predispose us to do things that end up looking downright foolish (with the benefit of 20/20 hindsight). Competing against well-armed professional investors is difficult enough. Add your own foibles to the mix, and the odds against developing a solid decision-making process look bleak. But if you want the upside of being a successful global macro investor, you need to find a way to ignore the noise—particularly the noise from inside your own head. How many investors, watching the stock market meltdown in the autumn, reacted in panic and sold their investments? Like many other investors, your instincts probably screamed, yes, *yes,* YES! But the logic of global macro responds with a firm no, unless all the data agrees, reassuring you this is the right thing to do. The essence of global macro investing is making fewer but more significant investment decisions. Sure, a small-cap mutual fund manager can pick the best stocks in his or her domain. But if that manager is convinced that real estate is a better bet than all the small-cap stocks out there, there is very little he or she can do about it. It's up to you and I to figure that out for ourselves. To manage that, all of us need to understand the ways in which our instincts will try to sabotage our better judgment.

For centuries, philosophers and economists have propounded theories of efficiency that govern both markets and men. In the case of market analysis, this peaked with efficient market theory, which I described in the first chapter. By 1970—decades before the phrase *insider information* became a buzzword—it was already clear that there were problems with this model. The Sage of Omaha, as Warren Buffett is known, once said, "I'd be a bum in the street with a tin cup if the markets were efficient." So Eugene Fama, a financial markets analyst at the University of Chicago, set out to find a way to adapt the model to the market's realities. He ended up creating three "substates" of the efficient market hypothesis. The "strong form" closely reflected the original thesis that security prices always perfectly reflect all the information that is available, both public and private, assuming a level playing field exists and that information flows readily from one group to another. Fama recognized the obvious flaws in that model. But the "weak form," which contended past prices and returns could be used to predict those in the future, was also weak. Technical analysts loved its deterministic nature, but technical analysis and the charts its practitioners rely on have their own flaws and inconsistencies. It's possible to link some behavioral trends (such as the visible reluctance of investors to let a stock fall below the point at which they bought it, most clearly seen when a recently public stock is hovering above its initial public offering price) to technical analysis, but charts can't serve as the basis for any solid investment program.

There are other, real-world, limitations on the degree to which markets can ever be utterly efficient. For instance, the efficiency theory assumes that all investors have a very long time horizon and that the menu of investment options doesn't change throughout. Both assumptions are flawed; no one's investment horizon stretches much past a decade (our personal and financial circumstances change too rapidly), while every decade seems to bring with it a new investment option that wasn't previously available. Those limitations help explain why the investment community now widely accepts Fama's "semi-strong" interpretation of the efficient markets theory and why it serves as the basis for most empirical economic research. This view acknowledges the reality that Buffett described: Pockets of inefficiency exist in financial markets that canny investors can identify and exploit. Increasingly, scholars who scrutinize market and investor behavior conclude that any gaps between a pure efficient market and actual price action can be attributed to human quirks. And the more volatile the market, the greater the degree to which human behavior and social psychology affect those markets. Understanding human psychology, in other words, can help investors develop an investment framework and process that stands the best chance of success. Only when we all acknowledge our own weaknesses can we rise above them.

Americans like to look on emotion-driven markets as something that we, in our collective wisdom, have left in the past. Tomes like *Extraordinary Popular Delusions and the Madness of Crowds*[1] remain big sellers, but most of us prefer to see phenomena like Tulip-mania as something of a historical curiosity. In fact, emotions still dominate intellect when it comes to questions of value, especially the value of something that we own (from a home to an old baseball card collection). All of us believe that our possessions are worth more than the highest bidder is willing to pay. I tested that theory—proving in the process the impact on our investment behavior—at a women's investment club luncheon in Ponte Vedra Beach, Florida. I asked the women sitting around each of the tables to compete against their neighbors. I began by asking each to guess the total market capitalization of the Standard & Poor's 500 Index. The winner at each table— the woman who came closest to guessing the correct answer—won the floral centerpiece decorating their table. In step two, I asked each new "owner" of the centerpiece to put a value on it, and asked her seven tablemates to do the same. Without exception, the "owners" decided that the centerpiece was worth more than twice as much as the highest price offered by the seven "bidders."

When this kind of distorted perception of value is transplanted to an investment process, it can lead to a kind of paralysis. Not surprisingly, that doesn't tend to produce solid results! Entire markets can freeze up in this way. Consider the real estate market crisis that began in 2007: As housing values declined nationwide, the inventory of unsold homes skyrocketed. Homeowners became unwilling to sell their property for less than they thought it was worth, while skittish buyers were unwilling to pay prices that they felt were unrealistic.

We all like to believe we are infinitely more rational thinkers than our ancestors, and we draw comfort in our self-delusion from the theories developed by economic philosophers like Adam Smith. Our favorite delusion—as spelled out by Smith and cherished ever since—is that when human beings are confronted with a set of facts, they will behave in the way best calculated to maximize their future financial security, physical safety, and comfort, a belief termed *unbounded rationality*. But individuals make decisions en masse in much the same way as the members of the Ponte Vedra investment club did individually when it came to pinning a value on a floral arrangement: They let emotions ride roughshod over rationality. At best, argued Herbert Simon of the University of Chicago (a pioneer of the emerging field of behavioral economics) in the mid-1950s, we may be able to lay claim to "bounded rationality." Emotions and biases constantly get in the way of making optimal investment decisions.

Back in 1999, two market analysts named Kenneth Froot and Emile Dabora decided to demonstrate how this worked in real life by studying the trading patterns of shares of two different sets of securities issued by Royal Dutch Shell. When the company was formed by a merger of Royal Dutch Petroleum in the Netherlands and Britain's Shell Transport in 1907, both companies agreed that the securities of the two companies would trade on separate exchanges. Royal Dutch, traded in Amsterdam, would be worth 60% of the new company. Shell, traded on the London Stock Exchange, would account for the remaining 40%. In a truly efficient market, the stocks should have traded at a 6:4 ratio, after adjusting for currency fluctuations between the Dutch guilder (later the euro) and the British pound. Instead, Froot and Dabora reported that they deviated from this relationship by as much as 35%. That can only be called downright *ir*rational. One possible reason for this is a psychological reluctance on the part of investors to abandon a market with which they were familiar and whose operations they understood, to transact business in an alien environment. The arbitrage opportunity—the possibility of buying the same thing for less money somewhere else—wasn't enough to compensate them for the psychological stress of leaving home. Puzzled? Think of the devoted Mac computer user trying to persuade his friends to abandon their constantly crashing Windows-based personal computers in favor of a Mac. Despite the PC users' technical difficulties, they dig in their heels; who wants to have to learn how to use a new computer system, even if it means fewer problems down the road?

Many investors have experienced firsthand the pricing anomalies that persist in closed-end mutual funds. (These funds have a finite number of shares, and an interested investor must buy those shares in

the fund from a willing seller; in contrast, anyone interested in investing in an open-end mutual fund can simply send money to the fund
company, which will issue new shares and put that capital to work.)
Because of its structure, the unit price of an open-end mutual fund's
shares tends to mirror the net asset value of all the stocks owned in the
fund's portfolio on a per-share basis. In contrast, as described in a
1990 study for the *Journal of Economic Perspectives*, three
researchers noted that the price of units in closed-end funds bore
little relationship to the net asset value of the underlying holdings.
In contrast to the flexible structure of open-end funds, issuing and
redeeming shares as investors demand, the share capital of closed-
end funds is fixed and finite. The researchers found the prices
investors were willing to pay sellers to acquire shares in those closed-
end funds had less to do with the net asset value of the holdings and
more to do with their perception of the type of fund. In other words,
sentiment triumphed. If small-cap stocks were out of favor with
investors, closed-end funds containing small caps traded below the
net asset value of their holdings—and the gap was wider than any
discounts applied to other closed-end funds. Meanwhile, open-end
small-cap funds continued to trade at or even above their net asset
value!

This kind of human irrationality can be seen throughout the
financial markets. This is why I am writing a book about the benefits
of global macro investing. Bottom-up stock picking and top-down
market selection are not mutually exclusive. You can certainly employ
stock selection as part of a global-macro approach. The issue is really
a matter of time and effort because if you can get market selection
right, then successful investing can be achieved with substantially
fewer critical decisions. After a quarter of a century as a professional
investor, I've come to accept that there is no way I can consistently
deliver top-quality risk-adjusted returns to my investors without
adhering to a rigid global macro investment discipline as part of my
strategy. I have to fight this on a daily basis, as I did when I returned to

Chicago after my trip to see the Canadian oil sands operations. I had to resist the stock's siren call. I *knew* that I didn't have enough insight into the company. Happily, I redirected my enthusiasm for Shell into an investment decision higher up that tree: I invested in a portfolio of companies with oil sands holdings. But every time I encounter an intriguing stock, I have to fight the same battle all over again.

The marketing hoopla that surrounds Wall Street conspires against us as investors—and if we listen to it, we will succumb to our worst instincts. On any newsstand, a dozen or more magazines offer an array of hot stocks or exciting mutual funds or ETFs. Mutual fund ads trumpet the stock-picking prowess of managers. Millions tune into CNBC, use online tools provided by Yahoo! or Google to compare stock charts, and ponder technical trading patterns. Magazine editors, television producers, and online site managers all know the truth: that their audience loves "news you can use." The phenomenon reaches its zenith with Jim Cramer, the hedge fund manager turned CNBC market commentator. Cramer is a Wall Street veteran who joined Goldman Sachs in 1984 and began picking stocks for his own hedge fund in 1987. And wow, is he entertaining, jumping around the set,flinging stuffed bulls and bears at his delighted audience. He rants about stocks—stocks he likes, stocks he loves, and stocks he hates— but nearly every day, it's a different stock. Cramer is capitalizing on *his* edge, his ability to grab your attention and turn you into an adrenaline junkie.

What would happen to Jim Cramer's ratings if he were to change his formula to concentrate on the relationship between large- and small-cap stocks? Picture it: "For 100 consecutive trading days, large caps have looked cheap relative to small caps! On a forward P/E basis, small caps continue to trade more than one standard deviation above their relative valuation range, but small-cap momentum remains powerful! I would like to see that momentum break down before I could recommend a shift out of small caps in favor of larger stocks!" Cue the yawns.

But there's a lot of money to be made exploiting the shifting valuations between large- and small-cap stocks. The problem? The kind of market trends that produce those returns for us can last 5 to 7 years without a major reversal. Consider the airline industry, an intensely competitive business where cash-strapped players jostle for a slightly smaller piece of a crowded market every day. When one player tries to boost fares by $25 to $50, the market watches to see whether other players match those hikes (and whether the market absorbs them). Gyrating fuel oil prices can wreak havoc on those airlines that didn't hedge their exposure to this cost, and benefit those who did. In spite of all its uncertainties, the airline industry still stands to benefit from any signs of global economic growth, so stock pickers looking for ways to "play" the theme of synchronized global growth may want to add an airline stock to their portfolio. But the best way to balance the risks of this move is to buy the sector and spread the risks. Only then can you lessen the company-specific risks.

The best-known piece of advice delivered by Fidelity's legendary money manager Peter Lynch is to "buy what you know." But his most helpful tip, delivered in *One Up on Wall Street*, is more thoughtful. Investors, he says, shouldn't just buy a single stock in an industry that appeals to them, but *all* the companies in that industry. That way, he advises, they stand the best chance of cutting volatility and reducing the risk of making a poor individual stock selection on inadequate information. That is particularly true in the example I gave you in Chapter 2, "The World of Global Macro," when the gains of one medical device company must come at the expense of a rival. But the same pattern applies even in industries like retailing, where income levels and the health of the economy is generally believed to serve as a rising tide lifting all boats. In fact, when I studied the performance of four of the largest retailers in the period from 1993 to 2007, the degree of divergence in the results astonished me. The best performer of the four was Kohl's, which posted an annualized 27.8% return, while Costco limped in with a mere 8.3% return. (In the middle were Wal-Mart and Target.) Every year, returns varied dramatically, with a median gap of 35.7 percentage points between the top and bottom performers—an immense difference. As ever, buying an equal-weighted portfolio of all four companies would have been the best strategy, returning an annualized 19.4% with less risk. And of course, as I've already pointed out, you only have to make and monitor one decision: whether the economy favors retailers in general.

Every 15 years or so, financial markets are rocked by the kind of violent waves of selling pressure such as that of the autumn of 2008. During that most recent wave of selling pressure, hedge funds and other investors who had relied on leverage to help them boost their returns were forced to sell whatever they could to meet margin calls or finance redemptions. Nearly all asset classes headed south in unison; conventional asset allocation, which relies on diversification as a hedge against losses, proved to be fruitless. Even investment-grade bonds—an asset class that rarely rises or falls more than a few percentage points in any given calendar year—plunged nearly 20% during the third quarter of 2008. Panicky or desperate investors tossed out the wheat with the chaff. The selloff created an array of unique buying opportunities in higher-quality asset classes such as investment-grade bonds and blue-chip stocks.

It may be this inherent optimism that leads even experienced professional investors to believe they can outsmart the market. Certainly, being a positive thinker might help get us through life with our sanity intact. Even medical research shows cancer and heart disease patients with an upbeat attitude have better outcomes or quality of life. Indeed, if we lose our confidence that the future will be better than the past, we forfeit our *joie de vivre*. We got a hefty dose of what a world dominated by pessimism might look like in the autumn of 2008, when Wall Street institutions began to topple like so many dominos, the credit crunch bit deep, and pundits began to draw gloomy comparisons with the 1929 stock market crash and the Great Depression. The money markets failed to function as panic gripped institutional investors. In one day alone, investors yanked more than $180 billion out of the stock market.

Conversely, an investor who is upbeat may become irrationally confident. Las Vegas's entire existence is based on that fact. Yes, the casino may always win in the long run. But why shouldn't I be the person who triumphs at the slot machine tonight? And if it doesn't happen tonight, well, tomorrow I may be luckier! The same spirit of unquenchable optimism possesses the stock market "gambler"—the investor who persists in acting on limited information and relying on tips and the opinions of others. Left unchecked, that kind of overconfidence will lead an investor to buy or sell based on a hunch or "feeling in my gut" rather than on information. In their 1999 study, entitled "Unskilled and Unaware," two Cornell University professors, Justin Kruger and David Dunning, asked a group of undergraduate students to predict their ability to recognize which jokes other people would find funny. On average, the undergrads thought they were pretty good at this; specifically, they put themselves in the 66th percentile. What's interesting about the study isn't whether they were correct in this assessment; it was the outsize confidence in something that wasn't in their area of expertise. (None of them was moonlighting as a standup comic.)

Alas, in people *with* some kind of expertise, self-confidence teeters on the brink of hubris. It's human nature; all of us tend to overestimate our skills. Why else would an overwhelming majority of those surveyed view themselves as "better than average" drivers? Let's be honest: Most of us reached our current positions by making good, profitable decisions in the past. (And therein lies another human foible that afflicts investors: the tendency to take credit for past favorable outcomes, regardless of whether our decisions had anything to do with the outcome, or whether we were just very, very lucky. That's the reason probably more than half of today's mutual fund portfolio managers believe they're better than the median.) Overconfidence may also make some pros overactive, buying and selling securities rapidly as their opinions fluctuate or as they respond intuitively to fresh news. The efficient market hypothesis dictates that investors should rarely trade, and yet more than a billion shares of the 30 stocks in the Dow Jones Industrial Average change hands every day. Some of the savviest veterans hold on to their stock positions for years at a time. Bill Miller, whose returns topped those of the S&P 500 Index for an astounding 15 years in a row, did so with an average annual turnover of only 13% in his fund, the Legg Mason Value Trust. That suggests that his average holding period is more than 7 years. In contrast, look at the myriad day traders who sprang up in the 1990s, making a living by reacting to each small change in a stock price by placing a buy or sell order. Few survived, and that approach to "investing" has been largely discredited.

The greater the trading volume and the more active the market, the more investors want to react. That's because many of us tend to view price changes as if they were infallible signals of some fundamental change in the securities we own. If the price changes, something must be different, we reason—and we must react. Of course, if you succumb to this urge, you are just generating still more market "noise." In 1991, Robert Shiller of Yale University surveyed the reactions of individual and institutional investors caught up in the stock market crash of October 19, 1987, when the S&P 500 plunged by more than 23% in a single day. Shiller found that investors who placed sell orders weren't doing so in response to any news event, other than the "news" that the stock market was falling. The dramatic drop in valuations became a vicious cycle, as one investor after another sprinted for the exit without bothering to stop and think whether any fundamental events caused the apparent cataclysm. As Shiller found, there weren't: Not a single piece of economic news existed that could have explained such a widespread selloff. For advocates of the efficient market theory, Black Monday is one of the hardest market events to explain, because there appears to be no reason for the selloff other than speculation, sentiment, and the "lemming phenomenon" of investors chasing after each other in the unwarranted assumption that the leaders of the pack *must* know what they are doing. Indeed, sellers on Black Monday turned out to be behaving in the same kind of self-destructive fashion as lemmings jumping off a cliff: It was investors who ran counter to the trend and bought stocks that day who emerged as the biggest winners. Any investor who had the foresight or fortitude to buy the stocks in the S&P 500 Index or an index fund on Tuesday morning, after the market had plummeted more than 20% the preceding day, would have scored a remarkable 15% return over the next 2 days (a coup by any standards).

The market crash of the fall of 2008 was, like Black Monday, one of the few occasions when investors found it easier to sell than to buy. In the midst of the incredible volatility in the Dow Jones Industrial Average and other major stock market indicators, anxious investors felt compelled to hit the "sell" button. Valuation issues had little to do with the rout; rather, the catalyst was the impact of lenders tightening their borrowing criteria on hedge funds already leveraged to the hilt. Generally speaking, however, we are financial pack rats: We buy and we hang on to our investments because we don't like to relinquish our winners and don't like to be forced to take a loss by selling our laggards. Psychologically, the pain of losing a dollar is greater than the joy of winning one. Suppose someone is offered the chance to flip a coin, and told that if it turned up heads, they will pocket $11, and if tails turns up, they will lose $10? Analytically, the odds are in our favor. However, most of us would pass up the opportunity to play because the chance of making $11 is offset by the potential pain of giving up our $10 bill. That might explain why, generally speaking, investors are so reluctant to realize their losses—even in the face of tax policies that allow us to use these losses to offset big realized gains elsewhere in our portfolios. It might also account for the kind of mass rush for shelter of the kind that occurred on Black Monday in 1987 and again in September and October 2008 when we collectively abandon hope that one day we will be able to show a profit on our portfolio.

The only way to protect ourselves and our portfolios from this level of irrational behavior is to establish a rational investment process that minimizes the opportunity for poor judgment, and to stick to it through thick and thin. As investors, we need to learn from Odysseus, who lashed himself to his ship's mast and stuffed the ears of his mariners with wax to resist the Sirens who lured mariners to their doom on nearby shoals.

The key to a rational investment process is to minimize the opportunities for our weaknesses to show themselves. A global macro decision-making process accomplishes this because it requires making fewer decisions and so creates fewer opportunities to be distracted. At the same time, each decision is likely to make a bigger difference to a portfolio. To build this kind of investment process, however, you need to put inductive reasoning front and center, because that relies on making independent observations before drawing a conclusion based on those observations. Perhaps one of the most familiar pieces of inductive reasoning is the following: All the crows I have ever seen are black; therefore, every crow in the world is black. In contrast, deductive reasoning starts with a conclusion, and then identifies data that supports that view (the kind of approach that Robert Gates once criticized me for following). Deductive logic runs as follows, in contrast: All birds fly. Crows are birds. Therefore crows fly.

As you can see, deductive reasoning holds many behavioral traps. For instance, an investment strategist may believe that energy stocks will underperform the market this year and find many pieces of data to support that conclusion. These can then be assembled in such a way as to generate a compelling story to which investors will respond with enthusiasm. The problem is the strategist's enthusiasm may cause him or her to overlook, downplay, or shun (consciously or unconsciously) contradictory information that doesn't support that conclusion. In contrast, an inductive process would have forced the strategist to consider many facts before reaching a conclusion. Let's go back to the crow example. Before stating conclusively that all crows are black, you might want to ponder the genetic makeup of crows to determine whether white crows are possible, or scrutinize naturalists' reports to discover if any have been reported. Inductive logic points you toward the conclusion but forces you to consider alternative scenarios.

Strategists, by nature, are confident professionals, most of whom have spent decades toiling in the investment business. Without incorporating an inductive process, there is no certainty that their future calls will be as successful; after all, those recommendations could be little more than emotion-based hunches bolstered by carefully selected and presented data points. And given the immense quantities of data available about anything you can imagine, it's all too easy these days for sloppy thinkers to start out with a hunch and find facts that support their theory. Nothing can illustrate the power of conviction more dramatically than looking at the mysterious case of the Hummer aficionados. A vehicle originally developed for military use, Hummers are gas guzzlers that hog the road, are hard to park, and aren't that useful. Still, Hummer drivers are die-hard fans of their vehicles and treat them almost as patriotic symbols. Even as the conflict in Iraq intensified and as gasoline prices soared, Hummer fans flaunted their vehicles. Eventually, the Hummer became exceedingly expensive to keep on the streets, and it wasn't until their pride rapidly eroded that some Hummer owners began to swap their prizes for environmentally friendly hybrids.

Inductive reasoning isn't infallible. After all, just because the only crows I have ever seen are black doesn't mean that somewhere in the world there isn't a unique breed of black-and-white striped crows flying around. I may never see one, or they may not exist at all, but it would be irrational to scour the globe in search of an exception to what has been an observable phenomenon throughout my life and the lives of everyone I know. Therefore, if the evidence supports it, I can reasonably conclude that it is safe to act as if all crows are black. Equally, it is reasonable to base investment decisions on data, or metrics, with a demonstrated ability over time to forecast a certain outcome. Adopting this kind of "bottom-up" approach helps me to remove raw emotion from the process. I can then make sound investment decisions by turning to indicators that have previously demonstrated their reliability. By so doing, I minimize my human urge to dig for data that supports a predetermined investment decision (for instance, the urge to dump my stock investments during a stock market rout like that of 2008 in response to what others are doing, instead of looking to see what the fundamental signals are telling me to do).

When you are in the midst of a massive market decline, the events are almost too traumatic to process immediately. That was certainly the case in September 2008 when the House of Representatives unexpectedly rejected a proposed rescue package for the banking industry in the wake of the Lehman Brothers bankruptcy. Instead of Congress resigning themselves to a $700 billion bailout package, investors had to suffer a $1 trillion loss in market capitalization, as the Dow Jones average plunged 8%. The move caught me completely off guard. I had been sitting in my office, writing my monthly newsletter to clients, when I answered the phone to a journalist asking me what would happen next. Next? Confused, I glanced at the stock quote terminal on my desk and was transfixed by what I saw: The Dow Jones benchmark had fallen 700 points. My first reaction was anger. Didn't Congress understand the gravity of the situation; the fact that if left unchecked, the credit crunch could cause the collapse of our financial system? I was angry, but also scared. A week later, however, I used the forced and panicky selling of the good, the bad, and the ugly in the stock market as a buying opportunity. The "good" stocks had been hammered so indiscriminately that they were trading at the same valuations as their "bad" and "ugly" counterparts.

To develop a process that will help you function in the midst of an emotional storm of this kind, you need to identify metrics that will help you single out the best opportunities in the financial markets while avoiding as many sources of risk as possible. Back in the final months of 1999, for instance, the stock market was in the final innings of the dot.com bubble. Many investors had drunk the Kool-Aid and waxed rhapsodic about a "new paradigm," while strategists who fretted about lofty market valuations found themselves fearing losing their jobs for becoming too bearish too soon. But investors who had kept an eye on the Federal Reserve valuation model (which measures the market's earnings yield against the prevailing 10-year Treasury rate) throughout the late 1990s would have noticed that by the fourth quarter of 1999 this critical fundamental signal suggested stocks were trading about 70% above their fair value. Although the degree to which that model signals the precise degree of over- or undervaluation might be up for debate, the sheer magnitude of the extent to which the market was out of whack made the model a valuable indicator. Indeed, it turned out to be a rather accurate tool: Over the next 3 years, the S&P 500 Index tumbled 33%, while the Nasdaq Composite Index plunged 56%.

You may find an investment approach that is based on numbers and sets of data feels boring at first. But it's far safer than chasing the "buzz" surrounding a single stock. Learn to be comfortable working with numbers, because building a solid investment process is all about finding the right sets of reliable metrics.

Endnotes

[1] Mackay, Charles. *Extraordinary Popular Delusions and the Madness of Crowds.* First published 1841; there are many reissues.

5

Identifying Metrics

In the 1920s, the great British mathematician G. H. Hardy paid a call on his ailing protégé, the self-taught prodigy Srinivasa Ramanujan. En route to Ramanujan's home in Putney, London, he noted the number of the cab: 1729. On his arrival, he noted to Ramanujan that the number "seemed to me rather a dull one, and that I hoped it was not an unfavorable omen" for Ramanujan's health. But the Indian mathematician—still seen as one of the world's greatest mathematical geniuses today—countered instantly that the number had immense significance. "It is the smallest number expressible as the sum of two cubes in different ways."

A few fortunate souls find numbers as easy to understand and manipulate as a high-school graduate finds the words in a first-grader's reading primer. When they look at a phone number, they don't see a series of random digits. Instead patterns combining prime and nonprime numbers take shape before their eyes. For them, conversing about numbers and their significance is as simple as chatting about the weather for the rest of us. Alas, most of us will never be able to compete in the International Mathematical Olympiad, much less win a gold medal or devise new mathematical proofs. With concentration and practice, however, you can toss your math phobia into the garbage, along with all the other bad habits that prevent you from making the best possible investment decisions, and embrace the world of metrics.

What are *metrics*? Really, metrics is nothing more than a fancy word used to describe numbers—specifically sets of data—to bring some kind of order to the often-chaotic investment process. Any time I sit down to analyze a prospective investment, a vast array of data competes for my attention: the stock's price/earnings ratio, its price/sales ratio, its stock performance relative to the industry or the market, the magnitude of the company's growth in profits and revenues in absolute and relative terms, the numbers of consumers lining up to purchase its goods or services, the economic trends that may affect those purchasing decisions. The list goes on and on, ad infinitum. And yes, these tend to be expressed in scary, jargon-filled phrases of the kind television pundits love to toss around to show how sophisticated and knowledgeable they are, and how plugged in they are to the wacky world of Wall Street.

In fact, metrics are nothing more than tools that enable investors to take raw numbers and express them in a way that tells all of us something useful about whatever it is they are studying. Without them, it's hard to make sensible decisions, since we would be operating in an information vacuum. For instance, when I turn the ignition key in my car, I start to rely on a series of data points, or metrics. When I pull onto the road and accelerate, my reflex is to glance at the tachometer to tell me when it's time to switch from first gear to second, and then to third. As I reach the ramp leading to the highway, I know that I can accelerate. As a sensible driver, however, I keep an eye on the speedometer to ensure that I'm not tempting fate in the shape of a traffic cop eager to nab me for speeding. And as I travel, I glance at my fuel gauge from time to time, keeping an eye open for a signal that I need to refill the gas tank.

The underlying principle behind financial metrics isn't very different from that governing the operations of a car's dashboard. Instead of relying on a series of data points to help me drive safely, I'm counting on different metrics to tell me what is happening in the financial markets. As I have discovered, finding the right pieces of data and understanding the signals that data sends gives me information about changing market trends (including when new trends are emerging). What kind of metrics you, the reader, find useful will vary depending on the investment decision you are trying to make. A professional options trader trying to decide whether to bet that a stock trading for $25 is likely to climb above $35 over the next 6 weeks needs to monitor data about stock price trends, volatility, and the number of days left until the various options contracts expire. Every day, quantitative analysts devise new ways of crunching through the seemingly inexhaustible amounts of data that Wall Street produces. One hedge fund manager has even found a way to analyze newspaper stories about stocks and—based on the frequency with which certain words and phrases appear—figure out whether the article is likely to have a positive or negative impact on the stock. Those calculations are run in fractions of a second on hundreds of newspaper articles every day, and then combined with more than a thousand other metrics to suggest tiny changes to the hedge fund's portfolio. Those calculations are run every 10 or 20 minutes, 24 hours a day, 7 days a week, 52 weeks a year.

Thankfully, most investors making long-term investment and asset-allocation decisions don't need to worry about building models that can tackle such outsize quantitative investment challenges. Rather than chasing every minute shift in the market and its individual components, you want to climb back up that decision tree. That, in turn, means identifying what pieces of data or metrics will help us make those top-level decisions: the macro investment bets. What are the building blocks that help *us* gain an edge in the financial markets?

I first started pondering this question when, after a brief stint as a quantitative analyst at Keystone Funds (a Boston mutual fund group that is now part of the Evergreen family of funds), I started working as a bond trader at Constitution Capital Management, the institutional investment arm of Bank of New England (now part of Bank of America). It was a big promotion, and meant I could stop transferring Keystone's investment data from handwritten green ledger sheets onto Lotus 1-2-3 programs on one of the first-generation IBM personal computers that were then the latest word in technological innovation. Instead, I would have the chance to manage a mortgage-backed bond fund. Gulp.

Suddenly, I found myself responsible for figuring out how consumers were likely to react to changes in interest rates; the rate at which they opted to refinance mortgages could have a dramatic impact on the value of the securities in my fund. In those days, before the 2008 collapse of Fannie Mae and Freddie Mac forced the government to nationalize the two lending agencies, I didn't really need to worry about my investors losing their principal. Still, as early as 1989, the mortgage markets had begun to get complicated, as investment bankers chopped up the principal and cash flow of these bonds, and then divided and reassembled them into new products known as collateralized debt obligations, or CDOs. These now-infamous new structures taxed even the most elaborate valuation models, and volatility increased. Even though the value of the mortgage-backed bonds was guaranteed by government agencies, investors didn't enjoy living through all those gyrations in the interim. They didn't want to cope with either big swings in their portfolio values or short-term losses. They were counting on me to do more than just react to the trends that would cause gyrations in the bonds' prices: They wanted me to *anticipate* those trends, and position the portfolio so that they would capture short-term profits as those trends unfolded. But that meant figuring out whether lots of homeowners would decide to renegotiate their mortgages as interest rates fell—causing high-interest loans to be repaid early. If so, no one would pay a premium for securities based on mortgages that carried above-average interest rates. The better I was at anticipating consumer behavior, the better my fund—and my career—would fare.

So I sat down and built a model, based on data sets and metrics, that anticipated mortgage-repayment behavior. I included all the available coupon and maturity combinations that were available in the mortgage market, and I updated it daily. There was so much data that the printout was about half an inch thick. Back in 1983, I had to run the program overnight because the computer's capacity was so limited and its processor so slow. Every morning I picked up the printout and studied the results—and acted on them. I had assembled the right sets of metrics and bingo! I had an edge in navigating the complex mortgage-backed securities market. During the 4-year period I managed that fund, I trounced my mortgage-backed bond benchmark annually, without taking on any interest rate risk. All I had to do was pick out the cheapest mortgage securities in each part of the market, buy them and hold them, while making sure that the interest rate exposure on my portfolio matched that of the index. It wasn't until an early Bloomberg data terminal introduced a similar analytical model that my edge vanished. At that point, anyone who could afford to rent a Bloomberg terminal had the same metrics.

Still, the message of how vital data can be stuck with me. That has become even more true as the amount of data available to us all has increased exponentially. As long as my analytical process is sound, the data I incorporate in that analysis is consistent, and the relationships are maintained, I know it's still possible for me to turn to metrics to help me develop an edge in almost any kind of market. For instance, as I'll demonstrate, if you keep track of the relationship between the yields on short-term and medium-term U.S. Treasury securities— what is known as the yield curve—you can obtain a lot of clues to the direction of the U.S. economy. For this to work consistently, you need to maintain the relationship. In other words, as you monitor the data and how it changes over time, you need to be sure that you are always using the same securities and maturities. And, as I'll show you when I tell you more about putting all these tools to work to build your own global macro process, you need to test the data to make sure that it remains effective. All you need to do is identify which metrics are relevant for whatever investment question you want to answer, in the same way that I check my speedometer when I notice I'm moving faster than other traffic on the interstate.

The first step is figuring out what you are trying to analyze. Is it the valuation level of the stock market? The impact of the economy on the bond market? Once you've done that, the next stage is deciding what data will help you answer that question and what weight it should be given at each stage of the decision-making process. It's easy, as I discovered to my chagrin when I was challenged for doing just this, to take a random statistic or piece of data and use it to produce (or rationalize) a buy or sell decision. But that's about as helpful as using a sledgehammer to crack a peanut shell, and just as counterproductive. You need metrics that will be appropriate.

Let's say that, because your portfolio includes some regional grocery and hardware retailers, you're interested in what's happening in retail stocks. You could study monthly consumer spending data. But if the companies you own do business mostly in California and the Southwest, then a recession on the East Coast that shows up in national data may not hurt your holdings. Or even if the downturn does filter through to the local economy, it might not damage purchases of staples like breakfast cereal or soup. So, you need data that is more regional, such as statewide consumer-spending data and store-specific results. You could develop metrics based on something like how many cars are parked in area shopping malls where your stores are located. How many parking spaces are available, and what percentage of them is filled? If that ratio has fallen over the past month, has a new mall been built that is siphoning off some business, and does that new mall contain the same mix of stores? You need to question any assumptions that you might be tempted to make. Perhaps the mall you are studying is new. In that case, the parking lot may be relatively empty simply because the owners built a large lot expecting to increase the size of the mall. There may be a smaller percentage of total parking capacity than at another mall. You may want to go further and study how many bags customers carry back to those cars, and what stores those customers seem to favor.

I'm not suggesting you should stake out your local malls; spending all your time counting cars and shopping bags can't be considered a great use of your time or give you any kind of 'edge' at all. Rather, I'm trying to give you a sense of the range of data available to you as an investor and the need to seek out what will prove most helpful. Metrics should be a tool, something that enables us to evaluate and compare one market or investment option against another in much the same way that Michelin's star rating system helps gourmets discern which restaurant is worthy of their attention. Michelin's reviewers don't just describe the meals they taste at thousands of restaurants around the world as "good" or "fabulous." They use stars as proxies for their ratings; a restaurant awarded two stars is worth going out of your way to get to, while the ultimate accolade—three stars—is awarded to a restaurant whose food is worth a trip in its own right. (When French chef Bernard Loiseau heard rumors that his restaurant, Cote d'Or, was in danger of losing its third star in 2003, he committed suicide.)

Luckily, the metrics that you need to build a robust investment process are more straightforward than is the subjective process of evaluating whether a particular restaurant's foie gras is delectable enough to command a premium rating. But it comes down to the same idea: Gourmets have their choice of restaurants; investors, their choice of what to put in their portfolios. If you don't invest your bonus in the precious metals mutual fund you're evaluating today, you're not going to stick it in your mattress. Instead, you'll pick another investment (alternative energy stocks, perhaps, or European bonds). A decision to opt for a particular restaurant or investment product comes with an opportunity cost. Deciding to go to that gourmet restaurant 10 miles away means you won't be able to try out the barbeque joint that has just opened down the road. You might pay more for your meal, wait longer for a table, have to change from your jeans into formal attire, and then drive through heavy traffic. Similarly, deciding to allocate part of your portfolio to gold and other precious metals means you won't be able to capture the upside potential in European bonds or technology stocks.

Metrics can help us decide whether those tradeoffs make sense. Just as Michelin's two-star rating may reassure diners in search of a good meal that their trip will be worth all the extra effort, so properly selected investment metrics used appropriately boost the odds of finding the best combination of potential risks and returns. In the investment world, the classic tradeoff is what is known as the *risk-free rate of return*. That term comes from the perception that parking capital in short-term Treasury bills is the safest investment out there; that is, free of risk, because the U.S. government guarantees those obligations (and the interest payments). That guarantee is at the heart of the credibility of the financial system; being even a day late making interest payments on Treasury securities would damage public confidence exponentially more than any number of bankruptcies or bailouts of financial institutions could do. (Let's face it, if the U.S. government defaults on its debt obligations, most of us will have much more to worry about than how our investment portfolios are performing.) As a result, these securities typically offer a minimal yield in exchange for minimal risk. At the height of the credit market panic in 2008, 3-month Treasury bills actually traded briefly at a negative yield, meaning that investors were willing to *pay* to preserve their capital, an indicator of how powerful this risk-free reputation is. Any investors who opt to put their capital in anything other than short-term Treasurys by definition will be accepting a greater degree of risk in the hope or expectation of being able to capture extra return. So their actual returns may usefully be compared against this risk-free rate of return.

Whenever you make an investment decision, you are really considering this kind of tradeoff between risk and return. The first decision that you make is likely to be whether you see stocks or bonds as offering the biggest possible upside. If you opt for stocks, the next question is automatic: U.S. stocks or foreign stocks? Let's suppose you prefer to stick with U.S. stocks. Immediately, you must make more decisions: large-cap or small-cap stocks? Growth or value? Using such a step-by-step process, you force emotion—the enemy of wise investment decisions—out of the picture altogether. You may feel intuitively that large-cap stocks, or some large-cap stocks, are attractive. But if you use the right metrics at each step in this process and end with the conclusion that stocks in general look less attractive than bonds, you would have to admit that buying large-cap stocks would be about as rational as picking investments by throwing darts at a list of stock symbols posted on a wall. Picking the right metrics and using them the right way in this kind of decision-making process boosts the odds that you minimize your weaknesses.

Each step along the way, metrics can help you shape your invest-ment expectations and clarify your goals. Picking the right metrics tells you how attractive each investment option is from a variety of standpoints. It's up to you to "fit" the right evaluation process and the right sets of data to the investment decision you are trying to make. Every piece of data won't have the same importance. You must iden-tify which ones are crucial, and which are just interesting or amusing. Suppose you were asked to develop a metrics-based method for eval-uating the success of that new barbeque restaurant. Some obvious data to monitor might include how long customers have to wait for a table, how busy the restaurant is on a typical evening, how many top ratings it receives from critics, and even how often its name pops up in newspapers or on the Internet as a celebrity dining spot. But if you fail to include some metric gauging how happy diners are with their experience (Are there enough servers? Do they get the orders right?), you risk missing an early warning sign.

Of course, data is far from scarce in the Internet era. Google the phrase *U.K. housing data,* and hundreds of Internet websites pop up, each offering different metrics on the housing market in England, Scotland, Wales, and Northern Ireland. One even provides an easily downloadable spreadsheet containing the average prices of housing in the country dating back to 1930. The challenge? Figuring out which data set will prove helpful in your particular quest.

Once you know what that quest is—what kind of investment decision you need to make, such as whether to opt for stocks, bonds, or precious metals—the next challenge is to take a 360-degree view of that decision. What are *all* the metrics that might exist that could have a bearing on your decision? Sometimes the challenge is sorting through a vast amount of data in search of what is most useful. In other cases, you'll need to assign a figure to a concept or variable, such as the level of customer satisfaction at the barbeque restaurant. Only after you've defined your task and identified the useful data can you begin to use it to reach a conclusion. Some decisions will be easier than others, because more data is available. If you're trying to figure out whether Russian or U.S. energy stocks are better investment bets, the lack of extensive financial data—and questions about its reliability—on the former will be a hurdle.

After you've assembled all the data you can, you need to evaluate and analyze it. In that process, reliability is a key ingredient. That means being aware of where that data came from in the first place. All investors are biased when it comes to deciding which sources are most reliable, just as all of us tend to evaluate facts or opinions depending on who provides them. For instance, many studies focusing on the way in which juries reach verdicts in criminal trials have shown that jurors place great weight on eyewitness testimony despite academic studies showing that such testimony is often flawed. (Eyewitnesses are notoriously bad at cross-racial identification, for starters, and many people take away wildly different impressions of the same dramatic but fleeting events.) Similarly, you may believe that government data is inherently reliable because you choose to trust in the authority of the government, or because you believe that the government is best positioned to capture the widest array of data. Here in the United States, data measurement has reached a fine art, but big swings are routine in such key sets of data as our quarterly gross domestic product. That figure is revised at least twice before being finalized—and then can be changed once more at the end of each year, when an annual figure is calculated. Elsewhere, government data may be still less reliable. In China, official GDP growth rates throughout the first years of the decade hovered between 9% and 10%. However, economists widely agreed that this data understated what was happening to the Chinese economy. Perhaps it would reveal how much inflation actually existed, or the magnitude of China's need for raw materials. An even more robust economy might also cause China's trading partners to press the country's rulers even more aggressively to allow the yuan to appreciate against the dollar and the euro (a move that would hurt China's export-oriented economy).

Adjusting data makes it more reliable—sometimes. For instance, data providers "seasonally adjust" construction or retailing industry data, as well as the prices of commodities like gasoline or heating oil. The summer driving season peaks between Memorial Day and July 4; in that period, gasoline prices also traditionally peak. New housing construction typically declines in bad weather and during the winter, so a plunge in housing starts in December can't be interpreted as a sign that the real estate market is in the doldrums. (It probably has more to do with the fact that builders can't dig foundations in frozen ground.)

One of the most common ways to use metrics is by referring to how a market benchmark, or index, performs. An index is just a basket of related investments. The granddaddy of them all, the Dow Jones Industrial Average, first published in 1896, contains 30 stocks that are industry giants and collectively measure what is happening across all major market sectors. When tracked historically, an index gives investors an idea of the kinds of returns they can expect if they invest in those securities. For instance, the Russell 2000 Index's performance will give you an idea of what you might earn—at least, on a historical basis—by buying smaller-cap stocks. It will also give you a lot of information about the nature and degree of risk you're taking, in both relative and absolute terms. Of course, indexes and their components change over time. When the Dow Jones average was created, it included stocks such as the American Cotton Oil

Company, the American Sugar Company, and National Lead. Now it includes four financial firms and three technology giants that didn't even exist a century ago.

The goal of anyone compiling an index is to provide us with a way to monitor a particular category of investment or asset class—large-cap stocks, say, or "junk" bonds issued by companies with poor credit ratings. Because each grouping is likely to react to a given set of economic data or other event in a similar fashion, because of their common characteristics, an index can serve as a benchmark. By comparing actual portfolio returns to that benchmark, investors can judge exactly how well they are doing, or how well a mutual fund manager is faring, relative to some kind of representative grouping of similar securities. As the array of possible investments has expanded, the experts of Wall Street have devised myriad new ways to slice and dice these asset classes into different categories, each one with its own index. Today it's easy to find a small-cap value stock index, or a large-cap Southeast Asian stock index. You can even find an index measuring the performance of "frontier" markets such as Vietnam and Kazakhstan.

In many cases, this proliferation of indexes has been helpful. While rising interest rates generally cause bond prices to fall (higher rates make lower-yielding securities less valuable), not all fixed-income securities will react exactly the same way to, say, a 1 percentage point rise in interest rates. Other factors, such as the currency in which the instrument was issued and in which interest payments are made, the duration or lifespan of the bond, and the credit quality of the issuer, may all magnify (or dampen) the impact of that interest rate change. So the experts crafted narrower benchmarks against which European bonds, Latin American bonds, investment-grade corporate bonds, junk bonds, mortgage-backed securities and asset-backed securities—among others—can be measured. Each investor or money manager can pick the index against which they want performance to be measured. A large-cap stock picker usually chooses the S&P 500, but a small- or mid-cap investor is more likely to pick a Russell Index, and perhaps even a growth or value subindex. If you're looking for some interesting reading, take a look at the quarterly fact sheet produced by a poorly performing mutual fund. In this marketing document (used to trumpet the manager's savvy and intellect), writers go to great lengths to not only rationalize the fact the fund is lagging well behind its principal index, but to downplay this in the way the data is presented. The marketing team will present the manager's returns for the 1-, 3- and 5-year period alongside those of the S&P 500, just as they are required to. But when that comparison makes the fund look bad, they'll go on to include the performance of a few other indexes—the Russell 2000 Value, say—against which the fund has done much better, and explain why that is really a better way to measure the manager's skill.

To be fair to investment managers whose investors demand that they not only keep pace with a given index but trounce it year after year, sometimes the problem does lie with the index itself. Occasionally, the metrics themselves don't really measure what they are supposed to, or what they once did. For instance, today's S&P 500 is a much different creature from that of 1999, when technology stocks dominated its returns and represented a whopping 33% of this common bellwether. That's because the index is "cap weighted": The stocks with the greatest market capitalization have the greatest percentage weight in the index. So, as the dot.com bubble inflated and tech stock valuations soared, so did the importance of technology in the S&P 500. As of the end of 2008, however, the index had only a 17% weighting in technology stocks.

Sometimes benchmarks become so flawed as to be useless. The Goldman Sachs Commodity Index, a basket of agricultural, industrial, and energy products, along with precious metals, was devised as a way to measure what's happening to the commodity universe—the world of hard assets. But it proved an unreliable indicator of commodity prices, showing very different sets of characteristics in the 1980s, 1990s, and today. However, those characteristics don't reflect any changes in the underlying market. Instead, the changes are attributable to the fact that the index was constructed without any provision for rebalancing it to reflect changes in the prices of individual commodities. Therefore, any outsize move in any single commodity (hardly unusual) permanently distorts the entire benchmark. There's no way to rebalance the weightings to reflect, say, the importance of each commodity within the economy or some other impartial metric; the commodity with the biggest price gain is assumed to be the most important. As oil prices quadrupled in the 6 years beginning in early 2003, oil has become a much bigger part of the index today than it was two decades ago. If that reflects oil's actual importance, it's only by accident. Goldman Sachs may claim that the index is a useful economic barometer, but its flaws make it an inadequate commodities market benchmark.

In contrast, the Dow Jones-AIG Commodity index is rebalanced each January. That means that it is a reliable metric, one that can be used as a basis for analytical models, because it is consistent and represents the real changes within the broad universe of the commodities markets. Useful metrics must be not only reliable but consistent; the greater those characteristics, the more weight you can place upon those metrics before making a final investment decision. Consider this, for example: If Michelin's analysts used their own standards to come up with a star rating, diners could never be sure that going out of their way to a three-star restaurant would always be worthwhile. So Michelin requires its reviewers worldwide to apply the same criteria to every establishment (although they keep the exact nature of that criteria as confidential as the reviewers' identities). Similarly, you want each investment decision to be reliable, so you must keep an eye on the consistency of your investment metrics.

Of course, Wall Street is anything but static. It wasn't until after the First World War that stocks joined bonds as a "mainstream" investment. Even then, it was only in the 1970s and 1980s that the popularization of mutual funds, combined with the shift from defined-benefit pension plans to defined-contribution retirement plans, made stock investing a preoccupation of ordinary Americans beyond Wall Street. As the size of these markets has increased along with the number of participants, so the diversity has grown. And the array of possible investments has exploded. An asset-allocation model that a decade ago might have been restricted to stocks, bonds, and cash could today include commodities, real estate, and private equity. Some of those markets didn't exist 25 years ago; others have undergone sweeping changes. As a result, metrics that were once useful may now be outdated.

The evolution of the emerging markets provides an excellent example of what happens to metrics as markets evolve. A decade ago, these countries had more in common with each other—their state of development relative to the rest of the global free market economy—than they do today. Back in 1996, for instance, the average correlation was 15%, meaning that for every 1% change in U.S. or European markets in any given direction, the emerging markets would react with a move of only 0.15%. Today, developed and emerging markets are more tightly linked; the correlation has hit 44%. That means it's harder for investors to seek shelter from the stock market meltdown in the United States in the emerging markets, even if the financial stocks in the latter remain relatively healthy. Moreover, that once-homogeneous universe of emerging markets is starting to fragment. Markets in Korea, Mexico, and Taiwan, for instance, no longer battle the lack of liquidity, the widespread corruption, and serious fundamental risks they did a decade ago. Rather, these markets have seen a dramatic improvement in credit quality, and many of their largest companies boast investment-grade ratings even as their national governments are becoming net creditors rather than debtors.

As the emerging markets category has evolved, new ways have to be found to reflect that a single broad index no longer accurately reflects what is going on within the asset class itself. For instance, one of the most heavily marketed global investing trends around is the BRIC phenomenon, sparked by a forecast by Goldman Sachs market guru Jim O'Neill when he forecast in 2001 that the BRIC countries (Brazil, Russia, India, and China) would dominate the global economy by mid-century. Standard & Poor's jumped on the concept, launching a new BRIC index, and investors have allocated billions of dollars to a host of new BRIC-specific funds worldwide. The market has acknowledged that the economic growth potential of these four economies has distinct characteristics from that of the rest of the emerging markets universe. Meanwhile, latecomers to BRIC investing are gravitating to the concept of frontier markets that remain full of perils for outsiders, ranging from Nigeria to Vietnam. Again, the argument is that these countries have more in common with each other than they do with others.

The bottom line for investors is that as the composition of the "emerging markets" universe changes and the correlation between it and "developed" markets increases, metrics once used to make decisions about whether to allocate capital to the emerging markets have become less consistent, less reliable, and thus less helpful. This isn't because of any inherent flaw in the construction of global indexes, however, but because the evolution of the markets themselves have made a broad global benchmark less useful. Standard & Poor's has pointed out that markets such as Korea and Taiwan dominate the MSCI Index (the equivalent of the S&P 500 for emerging markets investors, used to make decisions about the absolute and relative attractions of the emerging markets as an asset class). But the gross domestic products of these countries is tiny compared to countries such as China, and that gap is likely to widen. So perhaps the MSCI, which places more emphasis on the size of a country's financial market than the size of its economy, is no longer the most reliable metric for an investor trying to capture outsize returns as the next generation of emerging markets becomes mainstream. Maybe it's time to look around for a BRIC index. That is the kind of question investors must be prepared to ask themselves, in every market. Similarly, they need to question their automatic assumptions or biases about data. Anyone assuming that all emerging markets included in the MSCI benchmark must offer, by definition, the same combination of low correlations, high risk, and the potential for high returns would risk missing the reality. In fact, Korea's stock market, for instance, has much more in common with the S&P 500 than it does with that of Vietnam. The more I am prepared to question assumptions like this, the better I will fare in deciding what weight to give any given metric in a decision-making process.

Of course, because all kinds of data you and I use in our investment decisions is collected, compiled, and analyzed by human beings, it's hard to escape bias. Sometimes it's institutional. For instance, many indexes automatically weed out stocks that delist from an exchange, a process referred to as survivor bias. Others are either the unconscious byproduct of wishful thinking produced by an analyst deliberately donning rose-tinted spectacles. Did anyone really expect an association of real estate brokers to give you early warning that the bottom was about to fall out of the real estate market in 2006? Anyone who did was almost certainly late in recognizing what was happening. I have already discussed the most blatant kind of bias, the outright horse trading on the part of Wall Street investment banks during the 1990s in which analysts swapped favorable stock ratings for investment banking mandates. As a result, metrics based on a survey of the ratio of buy to sell ratings, or upgrade to downgrade ratings, or even analysts' earnings estimates during the 90s couldn't be seen as reliable, much less objective. Hopefully, the lasting legacy of the analysts' scandal will be the need for a greater degree of skepticism on the part of investors with respect to the potential for personal bias or conflict of interest in *all* the data they receive.

Yes, I demand a lot from the metrics I use. I have to. My investment track record depends on them. They must be an objective, consistent, and reliable way of measuring certain phenomena. And they have to be valid, in both an absolute and relative sense. To understand what I mean by this, imagine that I describe some one as "tall." In a vacuum (that is, without context), you have no way of determining whether my assessment is valid. Is that person a man or a woman, or maybe even a child? How tall am I? How tall are most other people in the room? To take that into the world of investing, consider one of the most widely used metrics in the investment universe: the price/earnings (or P/E) ratio. As its name implies, the P/E ratio tells us the relationship between a stock's price and its earnings by dividing the share price by the earnings per share. But the P/E ratio is a much fuzzier metric than that description implies. For instance, what earnings figure is used to compute the ratio? Some analysts use historic earnings per share (the profits the company posted the previous year), whereas others prefer to use their subjective estimates of what the company will earn this year or next. Let's assume that can be solved by insisting that P/E ratios be calculated in a standard fashion. Another hurdle appears: How is it possible to use P/E ratios in isolation and expect them to be valid? If Intel trades at 16 times earnings, is that good or bad? Unless you know the P/E ratios of other semiconductor companies, other large-cap technology companies, and the S&P 500 Index, you can't claim that is a bullish or bearish valuation.

Lots of metrics-related traps lie in wait for unwary investors. Sometimes relationships between a metric and an investment decision are casual, not causal, and deserve to be discarded or, at best, viewed as amusing but irrelevant. Figuring out which is which requires no mathematical skill whatsoever, but only a dose of common sense. For instance, we're all aware (thanks to Al Gore and *An Inconvenient Truth*) that global warming is heating up our planet and that the melting polar ice caps are triggering a rise in sea levels around the world, to the point where low-lying islands and nations such as Bangladesh find their long-term survival threatened. That's a causal relationship. Now, let's turn to the stock market, where index levels also rise and fall in any given year, but where, over a decade or two, the trend is for the value of the index to rise, notwithstanding the painful plunge in stock values of 2008. Hmm, interesting, isn't it? In fact, if you plot the level of the market and the level of the Atlantic Ocean on the same chart, you might even see a remarkably high correlation.

Whoa! You have just ventured from the territory of causal relationships into that of the casual relationship. Just because some kind of correlation may exist doesn't mean that the level of the Atlantic Ocean has anything to do with the level of the stock market (or vice versa) any more than global warming explains a multiyear bull market. Of course, this is an extreme example of the kind of silliness that follows if an investor starts treating casual relationships as causal ones. Alas, it's far from an isolated one. Every winter, for instance, as the world of football gets ready for the Super Bowl, CNBC is certain to start pondering, only half in jest, about what it will mean for the stock market if one team rather than another wins the game. That's because over four decades of Super Bowl championships, football fans doubling as stock market pundits have observed a pattern taking shape: Years in which a National Football Conference division champion has triumphed have generally been bullish years for stock investors. (The only exceptions were 1990, 2000, and 2008, when the Dow Jones Industrial Average plunged despite an NFC team's victory. With the victory of the AFC's Pittsburgh Steelers in early 2009, the stock market outlook seemed bearish for the year.) Add some common sense to this analysis, and you'll quickly conclude that football doesn't have a lot to do with the stock market. Certainly, any manager who admits relying on such casual indicators rather than sensible metrics is likely to see investors flee his or her fund as fast as possible!

Unfortunately, financial markets are chock-full of casual relationships. To make matters even more confusing, a relationship that once seemed to be causal can become less reliable and more casual with the passage of time. Counting the help wanted ads in major metropolitan newspapers was once a great way to gauge the labor market's strength because the data (the number of ads) bore a strong relationship to demand for workers and, by extension, wages, inflation trends, and corporate earnings trends. But the advent of the Internet changed everything. Employers and jobseekers alike turned to websites like Monster.com; fewer employers posted ads in the newspapers, and some stopped altogether. Relying on what those newspapers said, in isolation, would have produced a distorted picture of reality. That made the Conference Board's Help Wanted Index, based on those newspaper ads, less useful in anticipating key labor market data. The result? Today's traders, trying to "read" an early warning signal about a surprise change in unemployment or payroll data (which in turn might trigger big moves in stock and bond prices), have had to develop new metrics.

A more subtle consideration in selecting which metrics to rely on to make investment decisions is your time horizon. If you have a long-term investment timeframe—and as I'll explain, you shouldn't count on your decisions to translate into portfolio profits in less than 12 months—you don't want to be distracted by short-term data points. Over the shorter term, markets are driven by unpredictable, transient, and intangible elements that have nothing to do with fundamentals. Emotions kick in. A big investor might wake up one morning after a nightmare in which half of his portfolio was annihilated in the wake of an outbreak of nuclear war in the Middle East. Even though he realizes on a rational level that there is little likelihood of his nightmare happening, he believes he'll feel better if he sells 20% of his stock holdings and turns them into cash. The market reacts to his selling. Momentum takes over. Before you know it, you have a giant selloff. Massive, short-lived market movements have often tended to be unreliable indicators of long-term trends, although big slumps like those of September 1987 and the autumn of 2008 are painful to experience. In late February 2007, for instance, the Shanghai Stock

Exchange's index plunged nearly 10% in a single day. Within five months, however, the market had not only regained all of that loss but was up nearly 80% for the year. There may well have been fundamental reasons for concern about the outsize valuations and profits in the Chinese stock market in 2006 and 2007, but a single day's trading isn't the metric that will tell you what those are, or how to position yourself in response to them.

So an investor looking for compatible metrics needs to identify those that will be useful in making investment decisions over the next 12 to 18 months. Let's say you believe that investor sentiment is an important ingredient in deciding whether the U.S. stock market is a good place to be for that period of time. (As I'll demonstrate in Chapter 10, "The Fourth Factor: Psychology—Greed Versus Fear," metrics measuring investor psychology can prove useful in gauging confidence and enthusiasm and thus in making investment decisions.) The next step is to find the right way to measure levels of both fear and greed. Alas, many of the metrics most often used to determine investor attitudes to the market are too short term to be useful. Studying the weekly ratio of put options to call options, for instance, gives you information that is too volatile to be meaningful. Take a glance at a graph that shows the weekly change in the relationship between put and call options purchased on the Standard & Poor's 500 Index (options that give their holders the right to sell or buy the index, respectively, at a predetermined value within a defined period of time) and you'll see a sawtooth pattern. If you try to follow it that narrowly, your chosen metric will be sending dramatically different signals every 10 days or so! Any profit you *might* capture chasing these data signals is likely to be offset by your trading costs, not to mention the unquantifiable risks associated with sleepless nights. You need to find a way to look for bigger behavioral swings using the same basic data, ones that are aligned with our 12- to 18-month time horizon.

It takes a lot of work to figure out which metrics can be trusted to be consistently useful and reliable in any decision-making process.

But the effort doesn't stop there. You can never take for granted that the metrics you have settled on as the building blocks for your investment process will remain as reliable as they appear today. Just as every homeowner should periodically ask a surveyor to look for early warning signs that termites might be snacking on the wooden joists in the basement, so, too, investors must periodically step back and question the foundations on which their investment process has been constructed. Are the metrics still the right ones to use? Do they still send reliable signals about the same phenomena? As I have shown, correlations that have endured for decades may fade. For many years, investors who wanted insight into the course of inflation could look at the price of crude oil—an essential business input. Between 1986 and 2000, when crude oil prices rose, consumer and producer prices followed suit. But since 2001, the two sets of data have parted ways. Is this a permanent divergence or an anomaly? The answer remains unclear, but what is certain is that anyone counting on oil prices to predict inflation would have been drawing incorrect conclusions from that raw data and possibly have invested in securities and asset classes they expected to outperform in an inflationary environment.

In the words of Lord Kelvin, a nineteenth-century mathematician, "To measure is to know." Once you understand that the process of measuring involves the use of reliable and consistent metrics, it's time to start figuring out *what* to measure. What information is going to give you an edge? An investor's job is to determine which metrics work best at each step along the path toward an investment decision. The next chapters guide you through the process of breaking down seemingly complex investment decisions into bite-sized pieces and applying metrics to help you make those decisions successfully.

6

The Five Factors: Putting Data to Work

Everywhere you look, you'll find a piece of data, each bit of it playing some kind of role in your life. How cold is it outdoors? Glance at the thermometer for data. Now you know whether to don your thick wool overcoat. How much do you weigh this month? The answer tells you if you can afford to order cheesecake for dessert. Every day of your life, you absorb and process countless pieces of data, often without conscious thought. Sometimes those decisions involve processing multiple bits of data: Ordering the cheesecake may be a function of your weight, how much you can afford to spend on lunch, and how much time you have before you need to be back at your desk. But when it comes to building an investment process, you can't afford to handle data in quite such a slapdash manner. True, there's a lot of it out there, from stock prices and valuation ratios to pages and pages of economic information, including such esoteric details as changes in employment levels within Wisconsin's furniture-manufacturing industry.

"You can't manage what you don't measure." It's a hackneyed phrase because so many management gurus use it to describe the travails associated with running their companies. To discover whether their marketing campaigns are successful or a new business strategy is working out, business leaders and their senior managers must identify key performance indicators and monitor them. Investing isn't like managing a business, of course, but the adage can still help you make informed and rational decisions. The challenge is the same for everyone, as I discussed in the preceding chapter: Each investor must decide, independently, what he or she needs to measure in order to make a thoughtful buy or sell decision. I also have come to realize that just because I *can* measure something doesn't mean that the data I would produce is useful, much less significant.

That challenge of selecting and managing data is one that quantitative investors and money managers have wrestled with since the early 1970s, when technological advancements first made quantitative, or "quant," investing possible. The idea that an investment process could be constructed around sets of data rather than the results of in-depth research by individual investment researchers was still new when I joined Keystone Funds as a quantitative analyst in 1982. It was quickly apparent that, as a quant, I wasn't going to be part of the main-stream. The first task I set myself was to build a model that could tell me when stocks in the S&P 500 Index were over- or undervalued relative to their peers and to history. At the time, Keystone's dozen or so fund managers, along with another dozen analysts in charge of monitoring trends in various industry groups, preferred to focus on stock "stories" rather than on data. These stories revolved around some kind of insight into the company's business. A particular technology company was about to outperform, one analyst might argue, because it had slashed its debt levels and hired some brilliant new engineers to accelerate research and development even as the marketing was also gaining traction. Making the story better was news that the CEO of its chief competitor was trying to resolve a gender discrimination lawsuit and didn't have his eye on the ball. The role of the quants was to serve as a kind of chorus, providing data supporting that narrative.

That was the state of the investment world when I joined it. Back then, of course, developing and pursuing a pure quantitative investment strategies would have been prohibitively expensive because it would have required any company to purchase vast quantities of data and develop a proprietary database to analyze it. Only the major bro-kerage firms—Salomon Brothers, in particular—had both the financial resources and the conviction required to make significant headway in quant research. When I resolved to find ways to use data more systematically in my own investing, sorting through mountains of data in search of the handful of pieces of the puzzle that could be counted on to be consistently helpful and useful was frustrating. My very first valuation project showed me just how complex a task this would be. I decided that a good way to identify attractive stocks would be with some metric that would combine dividend yield (the size of a company's dividend relative to its stock price) and a company's historical stock price growth rate. With the right model, I could pick out companies offering an appealing combination of strong dividends and low volatility.

Because this seemed like a recipe for successful investing, I set about ranking the 500 stocks in the S&P Index each month based on this methodology. Alas, the data I selected didn't take into account everything that was happening in the market. It overlooked the fact that many fast-growing companies didn't pay dividends. (For instance, it would be another 20 years before Microsoft—one of the decade's biggest winners—paid out its first dividend.) A model based on dividend data that tried to identify the growth stocks most likely to outperform the rest of the market, it seemed, was inherently flawed. I would have been left with a portfolio stuffed with a bunch of boring utility companies and banks if I hadn't reconsidered my approach.

It was back to the drawing board, and to the seemingly endless and unmanageable amounts of data that the market spits out every day: intraday stock price moves and ranges; trading volume statistics; details on the number of investors selling the stock short (betting that the stock will decline); volatility; correlation (the degree to which one stock or market sector matched or deviated from its peers or the market as a whole); earnings results; dividend payments. It was enough to make a grown man weep. I was a victim of "information overload," the famous condition described by Alvin Toffler in his 1970 bestseller

Future Shock. Trying to grasp all this information made trying to take a sip of water from a fire hose seem simple in comparison. And as for trying to figure out which bits of the puzzle were actually *useful*...My mind boggled.

Happily, the process of managing raw data streams has become a lot simpler since then. Today, data that brokerage firms once treated as proprietary information is easily and readily accessible to anyone. For years, for instance, clients of Salomon Brothers received updates—in the mail—to the brokerage firm's Yield Book. Those updates ranked the various bond issues' yields by credit quality, maturity, sector, and other factors. Until the early 1990s, if I wanted to try to analyze this kind of yield information on a historical basis, I would have to send an assistant in search of the three-ring binder in which these updates were stored, and then someone would have to type each data point into a spreadsheet computer program (with all the potential for human error that involved). There was no way to do this on a time-sensitive basis, much less winnow out what pieces of data were important. Nowadays, data like this is only a mouse click away. (While I may access it on Bloomberg, you, the reader, can find much of the historical yield data or government statistics you need via the Internet at no charge.)

In the absence of hard quantitative indicators, and still looking for clues to market behavior in various kinds of data, I tried new approaches. By the mid-1980s, I was working at Constitution Capital Management overseeing bond funds for institutional investors such as pension funds. Finding ways to predict interest rate movements was crucial: It was the investment world's equivalent of the Holy Grail. That's when I stumbled over an interesting piece of data. Every week, *Barron's* reported the results of a survey by Investors Intelligence about the level of bullishness and bearishness in the bond market. One week I noticed that investors were rather pessimistic; only 35% of those surveyed expected interest rates to fall (sending bond prices higher) over the course of the coming month. Curiously, interest rates actually did fall over the course of that month. Hmm. To a natural contrarian like me, this data looked like gold dust. If I bought when everyone was bearish and sold when they turned bullish....

To build my model, I went from one stack of dusty old newspapers to the next, typing in the weekly sentiment figures. Every so often, a particular issue would be missing, leaving a gap in the data series, and I'd have to seek a copy elsewhere. Eventually, I had three years' worth of data, and, I figured, the beginnings of another data-based investment model. Alas, it was all in vain. It seemed as if investor sentiment wasn't a primary driver of the market's performance after all. Sure, it worked out some of the time, but not always. And I couldn't count on it in isolation. (Of course, in today's Internet era, I would have been able to build and test that model in a matter of a few hours before moving on.)

Still, by the late 1980s, life was getting easier for would-be quantitative analysts such as myself. Despite my failures, I remained sure that finding the right data and monitoring it actively would give me an edge in the markets. The problem was discovering what that data was and how to build the right model to use it effectively. Suddenly, Bloomberg opened its vast databases to clients, allowing users to download information onto their desktop computers to analyze as they wanted. Some major brokerage firms followed suit. Just as suddenly, I was able to access all kinds of fresh sets of data instantaneously. New research doors flew open wide. How did small stocks fare during periods of recession? All I had to do was sit down at my computer, clatter away at the keyboard for a few minutes and, bingo, I could tell you. Of course, I still made mistakes (there is a lot of truth in the old adage about models, "garbage in, garbage out"), but at least the process of trial and error was faster. It took days rather than weeks or months for me to discover there wasn't any pattern linking changes in companies' credit ratings and their stock prices.

Around 1990, I began to suspect my focus had been too narrow. I had been looking for ways to predict what was going to happen within individual segments of the market, or even individual securities. Every day, I showed up at work armed with the determination to beat the market by finding new ways to select individual bonds. But it was an endless battle, with very few victories on my part. Cheap bonds were usually cheap for a reason: Someone was dumping them onto the market because the company's credit profile was deteriorating. Even as I continued to hunt for another fraction of a percentage point to add to my portfolio's return each day, I grew to realize that a long-term investor's edge lies outside the daily frenzy of my trading desk. Even as I yelled and screamed and tore my hair out in frustration in reaction to the day-to-day bond price movements, a bigger dynamic was taking shape in the wings that would ultimately prove much more important to portfolio returns. Interest rates were falling, slowly and steadily. From 13.75% in June 1984, the yield on the 10-year Treasury note fell to only 7.375% by March 1986. Anyone who had done nothing but buy that benchmark Treasury and hang on to it throughout the long period during which interest rates declined would have walked away at the end of that period with a return of about 9% every year, on average.

This realization astounded me. While I had been running around in circles, chasing one tiny trading opportunity after another, I had missed the opportunity to put a single outsize trade in place, sit back calmly, and pull in the returns. All that was missing, I realized, was confidence in my own judgment. I would have to feel sure that I had correctly identified these major marketwide trading opportunities as they arose. But in the wake of this epiphany, it seemed clear that I needed to focus my research on identifying data that, together or alone, could tell me more about the direction of the various markets rather than the individual securities within them. If I could capture that trend, I told myself, the rest of the strategy would fall into place. But what I needed wasn't just ordinary data: I needed some superior form of data that could tell me what I needed to know about the bigger picture. I needed *factors*.

At the time, I didn't know what those factors were. In fact, the concept of factors, as they now appear to me, wasn't yet clear in my mind. Nor did I realize that I might need multiple factors to help me impose some kind of order on the investment landscape the way I wanted. It wasn't until I happened to pick up a copy of *Bloomberg Markets Magazine* one fall afternoon that the idea struck me. That issue contained a story that explained the basics of quantitative investing, and how these analytical techniques could help an investor better grasp what was going on across markets. It encouraged readers to think about financial markets from several perspectives simultaneously—with valuation issues and the economy among the key factors. Archimedes had his eureka moment in the bathtub; mine was more prosaic but felt like the same kind of breakthrough. It should be possible, I reasoned (still clutching the magazine in my hands) to assemble different data points onto a single investment "dashboard" that I could monitor on an ongoing basis. I had already recognized the need to step back and analyze the entire market. This latest revelation made me accept the logic that the key to understanding the markets, and thus to investment outperformance, lay in the interplay of multiple different factors. But which ones, and how did they work together? The article didn't give me many clues: It was an overview of sorts. But its author had given me a starting point. If I could figure out which factors were important and then determine which metrics would best shed light on those factors, the rest would fall into place.

My first goal was to identify a set of factors that might predict interest rate movements. I took bond yield data and compared this factor to others, including economic indicators such as GDP growth rates and inflation. To no avail; just as no single factor could help me, it seemed that factors couldn't be used within any single market to predict its direction. Fortunately, at around the same time (in the early 1990s), I moved to BankBoston, where one of my jobs was co-managing the 1784 Asset Allocation Fund. Working with my new colleague and friend Ron Claussen, my job would be to oversee a $50 million "balanced" retail mutual fund that kept roughly 60% of its assets in stocks and the remaining 40% in bonds and fixed-income securities. Like many bank-sponsored mutual funds, this product had been developed by BankBoston's Trust department for its wealthy clients. My job was to run the bond side of the portfolio, leaving Ron to focus on stocks. But it wasn't long before I began to think more broadly about the challenge the two of us faced. As its name implied, the fund's success hinged on the ability of its managers to decide on the right balance between stocks and bonds. Getting that right would mean that security selection—choosing which specific stocks or bonds to buy—would become easier. This was a way for me to test which factors enabled me to make that call, in what combinations, and with what level of consistency.

At first I settled on three sets of metrics, or factors. The first, which remains at the base of my investment model to this day, revolved around the market's fundamental valuations: The earnings yield model compares anticipated earnings (divided by the current price of the index) to the prevailing corporate borrowing rate. Because I knew that the economy was vital to whether stocks or bonds would outperform at any given point in time, for my second factor I turned to economic data, and specifically to data that would track the way interest rates on short-term and long-term securities shifted over time. The bigger the difference between them, I figured, the more likely that stocks would outperform, because the yield curve is good at predicting the economy's performance. Since investors expect higher interest rates to accompany economic growth, I could watch that yield differential widen as investors bet that interest rates would rise in coming years. Then I could draw conclusions about the implications of growth for both stocks and bonds.

I also believed momentum would prove vital in any decision to emphasize either stocks or bonds. Financial markets tend to keep moving in the direction they are going until new information arrives, attitudes change, or some other event forces investors to reconsider their opinions and change course. So I began to monitor the market's position relative to its 200-day moving average of the S&P 500, turn-ing bullish on stocks when the market traded above that line and bearish when it sank below it.

The concept of using quantitative metrics to manage our stock-bond balancing act took some getting used to. Ron was an old-line stock picker who relied on fundamental analysis, along with intuition. Then I arrived on the scene, an upstart from a bond-trading desk armed only with a mathematics degree and a lot of chutzpah. Whereas Ron's job was to select stocks that would collectively outper-form the S&P 500, mine was to buy bonds whose returns would trounce the Lehman Bond Index. But we needed to work together to decide on our asset-allocation target. Thankfully, Ron was open-minded and eager to explore any approach that might help us boost the fund's returns. Together, we refined my metrics process and inte-grated it into our decision making. The results were encouraging. Within 2 years, our fund was one of the top-ranked performers in its category, according to both Morningstar and Lipper. At last, I seemed to have achieved my ambition to apply quantitative measure-ments to investment decision making and shove my emotions govern-ing security selection to the background. Factors, it seemed clear, were the answer.

Of course, the process had to be refined on an ongoing basis. There was more to it than valuation and momentum, and my dash-board needed reconfiguring to reflect that. Ultimately I would decide that as well as market valuation, momentum, and the economy, I would need to track market sentiment and liquidity. These became my five factors. Encouragingly, all five worked most dramatically when applied to the big picture. Because that was where I already knew investment decisions could have the biggest impact on returns, as I explained with the decision tree in Chapter 2, "The World of Global Macro," I believed that my victory was twofold.

There were hiccups along the way, as in 1994 when these hand-picked factors sent me contradictory signals. I was sure that the stock market was going to outperform bonds that year. Valuations were reasonable, and the yield curve had an upward slope (meaning that longer-term issues carried higher interest rates and yields, a sure sign that bond investors were anticipating a period of economic growth ahead, during which stocks typically outperform). My momentum factor was also sending me the same message. But in March, the picture suddenly changed. Federal Reserve policy makers unexpectedly began raising short-term interest rates, boosting them from 3% to as high as 4.75%, sending stocks into a tailspin. Within 2 weeks, the S&P 500 had plunged 5%, leaving it below its 200-day moving average. Suddenly, our metrics were completely out of whack. What set should I trust? The valuation argument in favor of stocks was intact, but my momentum factor was now screaming "sell, sell, sell!"

I realized that my approach, of which I had been so proud, was incomplete. For starters, I was treating it as if it were a system: as if all I had to was input data points related to my chosen factors and the system would spit out the (correct) buy or sell decision. I had to face the harsh reality that there my dream was doomed. No electronic Wizard of Oz would emerge to tell me precisely and infallibly when to be in or out of the market. What I needed wasn't a system but, rather, a process. I knew that metrics could *help* me make investment decisions if I combined my factors with my own judgment and experience. Metrics made sense, but not in isolation. So I set out to refine the framework and review what factors would work best within this new approach.

Clearly, valuation had to remain at the heart of that process. Without examining valuation, it isn't possible to even try to decide whether a market is attractive on an absolute or relative basis. This factor is at the core, one way or another, of nearly every investment decision made today. Someone who decides a particular stock is cheap and a "good buy" is making that call based on valuation. So, too, are those whose quantitative model tells them it's time to shift assets out of overvalued U.S. small-cap stocks and into undervalued emerging-market bonds. Of course, every factor, including valuation, can and should be second-guessed. For instance, a key valuation metric is data that aggregates the opinions of investment research analysts' regarding corporate earnings. Do they expect stocks to post higher or lower earnings results over the next 4 quarters, and what is the magnitude of that forecast gain or loss? Obviously, a shrinking rate of growth or a shift from positive earnings growth to losses would be bearish signals. But all of that hinges on the reliability of those earnings forecasts.

At the beginning of 2008, a lot of attention was placed on what analysts were thinking about earnings as the real estate market's woes spilled over into the stock market and economists debated the likelihood of a recession. By January, economic indicators were predicting a bleaker environment than most pundits had expected. But with the collection of analysts who followed individual companies or industries at that time, most seemed to be living in some kind of parallel universe, one where the economic sun shone brightly and earnings were expected to soar. Indeed, just weeks before the government issued a bleak fourth-quarter GDP report, analysts were calling, in aggregate, for a 15%-plus jump in corporate earnings! Something was clearly amiss; one of these groups had misread completely the economic environment.

When I looked at data from Ned Davis Research, which has studied the behavior of corporate earnings in a variety of economic contexts, managing this conflict became easier. That data suggests that during times of recession, when the rate of GDP growth declines, corporate earnings tend to fall at an annualized rate of 5%. But only experience can help you know how to interpret and second-guess the behavior of the industry analysts and find ways to adjust your own strategy in response. Most of the time the input data I use is fine, but I know that sometimes I need to circle back and check to see whether it's reasonable. It's the same process as my 11-year-old daughter follows when she tries to solve a story problem about a boy walking around town and comes up with an answer of 510 miles. Odds are that answer is unreasonable and she'll have to sharpen her pencil and take another crack at her calculations.

When it comes to the investment markets, sometimes interest rates, particularly Treasury yields, move for reasons that don't have that much to do with economic trends. As recently as 2002, for instance, the yield on the 10-year Treasury note declined in spite of aggressive Fed action. By February 2005, a confused Alan Greenspan admitted the fact that yields on 10-year Treasury securities kept falling even as he and fellow Federal Reserve policy makers kept raising short-term rates was a "conundrum." What Greenspan didn't realize was that the real reason for the sharp slide in Treasury yields had nothing to do with the economy and everything to do with a buying spree by foreign central banks and institutions from countries such as China and India. All these trading partners were coping with their own glut of savings by using them to buy all the U.S. Treasury securities they could lay their hands on. As happens whenever demand for a commodity spikes unexpectedly, the price also spiked, sending yields lower. This enormous flow of funds resulted in artificially low interest rates and, as a result, pushed domestic lenders to take on more risk to maintain their lending targets. Incidentally, this flood of cheap capital helped fuel the housing bubble that, in turn, was largely responsible for the market meltdown of 2008.

Obviously, the factors that collectively represent an investment process—and the elements they contain—can never be frozen in time. They are inherently dynamic, as I realized in 1994 when the sudden jump in interest rates made me understand that I needed to include liquidity as a factor in my investment model. The spike in short-term lending rates that I have already described made capital instantly more costly and scarce and made liquidity a crucial factor. By ratcheting up interest rates, the Fed was able to transform a market with ample liquidity (and positive stock market fundamentals) into one where a shortage of investment capital and a reluctance to put that to work in any risky investment translated into a bear market for stocks. Clearly, I needed to find metrics that would help me track this important factor.

It wasn't until the late 1990s that psychology emerged as my fifth factor. Until then, I had viewed market psychology as something that provided headlines for journalists but not much useful data for professional investors. It was sometimes intriguing but rarely relevant. But after I started working for the wealthy clients of a private bank, my views began to change. For these wealthy families, the money I managed was *their* money, a symbol of their success. For the first time, I found myself understanding in a real sense just how an individual investor's emotions can wreak havoc on rational decision making.

It took more than a decade, but by the late 1990s I was close to refining my personal version of the Holy Grail: a quantitatively based investment process. It was clear to me that five factors need to be considered by anyone hoping to develop a process that is both robust and successful. Collectively, valuation, the economy, liquidity, investor psychology, and momentum explain and shape a good deal of the major movements within financial markets. The weight of any single factor might vary from time to time, but investors who make their market selections based on all five factors are likely to end up with a stronger portfolio, one characterized by higher returns and lower risk levels.

That isn't to say that understanding these factors, monitoring the data sets associated with each, and analyzing the results is always simple and straightforward. On the plus side, obtaining the data is a simple matter, especially compared to two decades ago when I started trying to do this. The Internet has decisively leveled the playing field, making all the data investors may need available at the click of a mouse (as readily available to the part-time investor monitoring his own retirement funds as it is to pension fund trustees or hedge fund managers who devote all their waking hours to the markets). Implementing those decisions has also become much simpler. By emphasizing factors that point investors toward the kind of major turning points in financial markets, the process steers you directly toward the kind of simple yet high-impact decisions that all of us should favor in our portfolios. Listen to what the five factors tell you about the markets and you'll be able to step back and wait patiently for that handful of trading opportunities that offer true upside potential to appear.

Note the use of the word *wait*. Building and overseeing your own investment process based on the five factors isn't going to be nearly as exciting as stock picking can be. And it requires patience. You will need to look at or gather data at regular intervals (every month, at least), and then evaluate it. But those evaluations should be made with a 12- to 18-month investment horizon. Sure, some investments pay off much more quickly. We all read about them in the newspapers. But the reason we read about them is because of their rarity; newspapers don't celebrate routine events. (That's while you'll never see a headline that reads "12,327 planes landed safely yesterday.") Alas, quick returns usually go hand in hand with an outsize degree of risk and inevitably with high volatility. So an overnight investment triumph isn't likely to help you sleep more peacefully.

The key to any global macro approach is the quest for markets that are either relatively cheap or relatively expensive. That is what the five factors that I have identified and that I explain to you in the coming chapters are designed to do. However, valuation changes for whole asset classes or asset categories, such as bonds or large-cap stocks, don't occur as rapidly as those for individual stocks. Just because your research steers you toward a particularly cheap asset class, there is no guarantee that other investors will follow your lead and start hitting the "buy" button themselves. Instead of expecting instant gratification, you should prepare for frustration as weeks and months pass before the market gradually comes around to the same point of view. All things being equal, expensive markets tend to become more pricey, while the relative bargains you have discovered become even bigger bargains as their valuations slump further. It's the classic conundrum that all value and contrarian investors must understand and accept.

To pursue a factor-based global macro strategy successfully, you must learn to be disciplined. That means recognizing that you might never buy at the lowest possible price and learning to be content with the fact that you picked up a *relative* bargain. Remind yourself as often as you need to that it is over periods of 12 to 18 months or longer that cheap markets tend to outperform their more expensive counterparts. Need proof? Just look back to the years from 2002 to 2006, a period during which the Russell 2000 Index outpaced the S&P 500. Of course, some of that move was rational and supported by the fundamentals. Still, by late 2004, the price/earnings ratio of the smaller stocks in the Russell benchmark exceeded that of the large-cap stocks in the S&P 500. That prompted strategists to declare (prematurely) that the small-stock rally was about to end. Instead, smaller stocks continued to beat their blue-chip counterparts until April 2007. Investors who reacted to the signal sent by one set of metrics—the valuation factor—would have seen their patience rewarded eventually. But those investors would also have had to deal with a lot more angst than someone who had waited until more factors were in place.

Heading into the discussion of the five factors, I can promise you that you will *not* experience all the excitement and drama you may have seen watching CNBC. Hopefully, the market meltdown of the autumn of 2008 has left you with an aversion to "thrills" of that kind, and that you have been left instead with a willingness to be patient and tolerate short-term frustration in the pursuit of long-term gains. Major market shifts don't happen overnight, and they don't happen every 3 months or so. A factor-based approach can be about as exciting and drama-filled as watching paint dry. When it comes to investing, however, as recent events have shown, excitement can also be perilous. Incorporating a global macro process will leave you with a healthier portfolio.

Now it's time to investigate the inner workings of each of these factors. Over the next five chapters, I'll help you understand how to think about each of them and how to tackle your most important job as an investor: discerning what each can say about the markets and understanding how to look at the data sets that collectively make up each factor.

7

The First Factor: Momentum— Befriending the Trend

If there is one thing that Wall Street loves to do, it's coin an adage. "Don't fight the Fed!" some market veterans will chide. "Don't fight the tape!" others caution, referring to the long strips of paper containing stock quotes that once spewed out from what was known as the "ticker" in the days before computers made obtaining the latest share price data as simple as clicking a mouse. When markets are particularly volatile or heading south rapidly, cheap markets tend to get cheaper. That's why the mantra "the trend is your friend" has become the most widely used (or overused) catchphrase on Wall Street.

What these phrases share is a focus on momentum, and specifically the need to be cautious about investing when momentum dominates financial market activity. Remember the old Road Runner cartoons that all of us watched on Saturday and Sunday mornings? As Road Runner zipped along the roads at the speed of light, the hapless Wile E. Coyote sped after him in an endless and fruitless quest to catch his prey. In each episode, there was always one moment when Wile E. Coyote became so carried away with his pursuit of Road Runner that he doesn't realize his mad rush has carried him over a cliff. Only when it's too late does it dawn on him that there is no solid ground underneath his paws. He tries to run faster, in a vain bid to get back to the roadway, but instead plunges to the bottom of the canyon. The triumphant Road Runner carries on his way with a jubilant "beep-beep."

Dealing with our first factor, momentum, can be just as tricky as chasing Road Runner. As all the Wall Street mantras imply, trying to bend momentum to our will can lead us to disaster in just the same way that the Wile E. Coyote's reckless pursuit leads him over the cliff edge time after time. (Alas, the damage you can do to your portfolio in the process isn't usually as quickly repaired as that to the fictional Wile E. Coyote, who miraculously reappears intact in the next episode.) Ignoring it is foolish; getting carried away with it is also hazardous. So what if the trend is our friend? As my mother never stopped telling me, "If your friend jumped off a cliff, would you do that too?"

Trends dominate financial markets, and momentum shapes those trends. Befriending a trend doesn't mean following it blindly. Rather, you must recognize the point at which that trend is old and about to shift gears, alter direction, or simply vanish altogether. Year in and year out, economists and investment pundits deliver a steady stream of forecasts that one trend or another is about to end. It's always something dramatic, because telling readers or viewers that financial stocks are still in the doldrums isn't going to appeal to them. Rather, it's the *new*, new thing that grabs their attention. Logically, then, the soothsayer who is predicting something downright bizarre—say, that the Dow Jones Industrial Average is about to double—will get the most media attention, as long as he or she can put forward a logical argument in support of that prediction. Take a look at the overstock table in a bookstore sometime, covered with the unsold and outdated hardcover books that once were trumpeted as the season's must-read works. There you'll find, gathering dust, provocative titles such as *Dow 40,000: Strategies for Profiting From the Greatest Bull Market in History*, by David Elias, published in June 1999. As we all recall, less than a year later, investors were reeling from the implosion of this greatest bull market; a decade later, the Dow was further from, rather than nearer, that 40,000 mark. Then there was *Bear Market Investing Strategies*, by Harry D. Schultz. Ironically, it was first published in July 2002, months before the start of a 5-year bull market. So much for capturing the trend.

Once you start thinking about all the competing arguments pundits make in favor of their pet trends, you'll probably start to realize just how many flawed prophets there are out there. Throughout 2005 and 2006, for instance, scores of analysts predicted the imminent demise of the small-cap rally. Nevertheless, as I discussed in the preceding chapter, small stocks continued to outpace the S&P 500 month after month until early 2007. I confess that I've occasionally been caught up in the temptation to call for the end to a trend, predicting, for instance, that real estate investment trusts (REITs) would lag in 2005 and 2006. Alas, being early is just another way to be wrong in the financial markets. Even the most experienced and successful investors end up dismayed and baffled by the continued *out*performance of an asset class or category that they firmly believe is poised for a cyclical slump or that is overvalued.

In fact, trends are much more powerful, resilient, and long-lasting than we like to admit. That means investors are tempted to make two different kinds of asset-allocation errors, both of which undermine our ability to make solid investment decisions. One of the most common is the one I have already referred to. The longer a rally continues, the more overstretched valuations become, the more nervous I know that I become, and the more likely I am to unilaterally decide that the rally is over (long before the trend itself is ready to give up the ghost). Or else we stay too long at the party and end up bleary-eyed and hung over, cleaning up after everyone else has gone home. Market trends may excite human emotions in investors, but they don't respond to those emotions. Cheap markets get cheaper, bull markets drag on and on. Make a move out of impatience, and the price you pay could be a high one. Back in early 2005, the real estate market's fundamentals made REITs look like a costly and risky investment. Yields on publicly traded real estate trusts, a key valuation indicator, had fallen to historic lows relative to 10-year Treasury notes. But the positive momentum still ruled the day. The Bloomberg index of REITs climbed 11.6% in 2005 and soared another 33.9% the following year. It wasn't until 2007 that the valuation issues finally interrupted the momentum.

Any model that emphasizes other factors, even such a crucial one as valuation fundamentals, at the expense of momentum is one that contains a fatal flaw. Yes, other factors can draw your attention to a potential problem, but it's the momentum factor that will tell you about the timing of a correction or rebound. *Mis*reading a momentum indicator is just as perilous as overlooking momentum altogether. Anyone who decided in early 2000 that the momentum of the previous few months would continue into the spring and summer paid a heavy price when the dot.com bubble finally burst, just as anyone who responded to Fed Chairman Alan Greenspan's warning about "irrational exuberance" in late 1996 would have forfeited 3 years of rich stock market returns. So the key to being a successful global macro investor is buying markets when they are cheap and about to increase in value, while shunning those that are costly and about to see valuations contract. Of course, you need other factors, notably valuation fundamentals, to help you distinguish which markets are which. But only momentum can help you with the second step: figuring out when those valuations are about to change and adjusting your portfolio accordingly.

If you have a broker or financial advisor helping you with your investment portfolio, he or she probably reminds you a lot—especially during bear markets—that you need to be invested in stocks most of the time. History has shown that about 30% of a bull market's move occurs in the first three months of a rally. Being late to the game can cost you massively in terms of foregone profits. But even the most skilled investors have demonstrated over and over again that they can't predict when a market is about to shift directions. That's one reason why pundits refer scathingly to "market timing" as a strategy doomed to fail. Another reason for staying invested in the market is that uptrends in stocks tend to last longer than downtrends. Over the past 50 years, the 30 stocks in the Dow Jones Industrial Average posted gains in 129 quarters but only lost ground in 74 quarters. If you've just experienced one positive quarter, there is a 53% chance that the next will also be profitable, according to historical models. What makes it tough for investors to stay put, and the reason that your adviser probably has to prod you to do so, is that the quarters in which market indexes fall are painful to endure. Yes, the typical downtrend may be rare and short-lived, but it's also more pronounced than are the gains in the positive quarters. (Optimism and enthusiasm take months or years to manifest themselves; panic can develop overnight.) Of the five 3-month periods in which the Dow benchmark has been most volatile over that 50-year period, three of them saw big downward movements. The worst? Not surprisingly, it was the fourth quarter of 1987, during which the Dow plunged an astonishing 25.3%. (The autumn of 2008 may have felt worse to investors who don't have a firsthand recollection of 1987, but in fact, the Dow slid less than 18% in the third quarter of that year.)

Let's say that all the other metrics you study are telling you a bull market is getting a bit long in the tooth or that a valuation gap that has existed between two asset classes is about to correct itself. Naturally, you're eager to jump in and take a position to profit from that over-or undervaluation; that's human nature. Before you act, however, ask yourself whether you're about to behave like a cartoon coyote, ignoring the rules of momentum and ending up splattered on some canyon floor. Instead, you need to find a way to work with a trend that you identify. If you develop and use a set of momentum-based metrics, you will be able to pick your entry point more astutely, or identify the moment when it is prudent to head for the exit. If you manage those momentum indicators properly, you'll equip yourself with a virtual set of brakes: Even if you find that a market in which you have invested no longer has any visible means of support, you'll be able to slow down and shift direction in time to avoid heading over the cliff.

Momentum is the link that connects theory with reality. Investors can develop a theory that a particular market is expensive and over-priced, drawing on information provided by the other four factors.

But that conclusion about valuation is still only theoretical. It becomes relevant—and something that you should act on—only when perception becomes reality. When investors aren't just worrying about a market being risky but seeking shelter by selling, you are dealing with reality. The momentum has shifted. If you grasp the momentum factor, you will be able to determine when to act, and be aware of exactly how rapid or forceful a particular change in market direction seems likely to be.

The ultimate trend junkies are technical investors, so some of the momentum metrics you might find yourself using are the stock price charts and other tools that these folks employ with an almost religious zeal. Technical analysts, however, tend to ignore other factors. I believe you need to steer a middle course; adopting some key technical models to help you grasp the momentum trends, without shunning or discounting what other factors are telling you. Perhaps the most important of the weapons in a technician's arsenal is the 200-day moving average. This is generally viewed as the dividing line that tells you when a stock or index looks healthy on a technical basis and is calculated by determining an average of all the prices for a stock (or bond, or index) for 200 trading days in a row. (That roughly equals a full calendar year of trading days.) Then the stock's current price is compared to where it has been over that 200-day period. Let's say that other factors are telling you that small-cap stocks are a roaring "buy." If the Russell 2000 Index (or any other proxy for small-cap stocks that you choose) is trading above its 200-day moving average, I think that's a reliable signal that it's time to shift assets into smaller stocks. As long as the index level remains above its 200-day moving average, the bullish trend is intact. When it falls below that line, that serves an equally reliable "sell" indicator.

This tool is so useful that even if you don't look to other metrics for confirmation, it can prove very helpful. In one study that my team conducted at Harris Private Bank, we discovered that an investor relying on the signals sent by this 200-day moving average would have fared better than another one who just followed the advice to "buy and hold." Specifically, someone who began investing in December 1980 and bought stocks in the Dow Jones index whenever it traded 1 percentage point above its 200-day moving average, and sold them whenever it dipped 1 percentage point below that average (putting the proceeds in some other kinds of securities yielding an average of 4% a year), would have had, by December 2008, $1,681 for every $100 he had started with. The buy and hold investor, in contrast, would have ended with $890 for every $100 invested (see Figure 7.1).

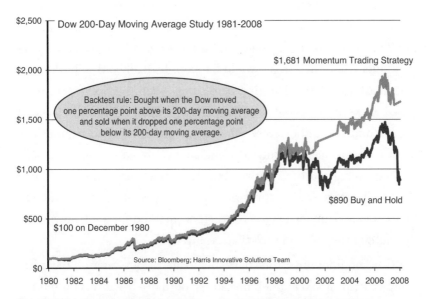

Figure 7.1   Buy and hold investing versus momentum investing.

Moving averages are just as useful when you want to compare one market against another as they are in identifying entry and exit points in any single market. However, relative market trends tend to last a lot longer than individual market trends. So when you're trying to understand whether smaller stocks are a better buy than their large-cap counterparts—rather than just trying to pick the right time to buy small caps—you need to use metrics based on longer time periods. For instance, between late 1999 and 2006, investors who bought the small-cap stocks in the Russell 2000 Index earned returns that were

80 percentage points higher than those they would have captured investing in the large-cap universe as represented by the S&P 500. (Over that time frame, the S&P 500 advanced a measly 24.2%, while the Russell 2000 surged 104.9%, including dividends.)

As I've noted, pundits were particularly eager to call an end to that long-lasting trend. Ultimately, small stocks (as represented by the Russell 2000 Index) sported a price/earnings ratio that was an astonishing eight times that of those in the S&P 500. Small-cap stocks seemed to defy the laws of gravity, or at least the rules that said big valuation gaps should narrow rather than become larger. But studying the 20-month moving average would have helped an investor trying to predict when that break would happen. It finally did so in the second quarter of 2007. The first clue came when the S&P 500 finally broke above its 20-month moving average. That mirrored what had occurred in December 1999, when small-cap stocks had begun their period of spectacular outperformance by breaking the 20-month moving average of the relative return between large- and small-cap stocks. The stage was set for large caps to outperform, a phenomenon that remained intact even as the stock market spiraled downward throughout the autumn of 2008 (see Figure 7.2).

Commodities investors have been far bigger fans of technical analysis than stock market investors, perhaps because commodity price trends tend to persist longer than those in other markets. Evaluating the Dow Jones Commodity Index between March 1991 and March 2008, my research team found that the odds of one positive quarterly return being followed by another were 59%, whereas the likelihood that one money-losing quarter would be followed by another was only 39%. Obviously, momentum is a powerful force in commodities markets, and timing is crucial, so the momentum factor can have a particularly dramatic impact on these returns. For instance, an investor who used the 52-week moving average in the same way that I've outlined above (buying and selling when the prevailing price of the CRB index—the commodity market's benchmark—was

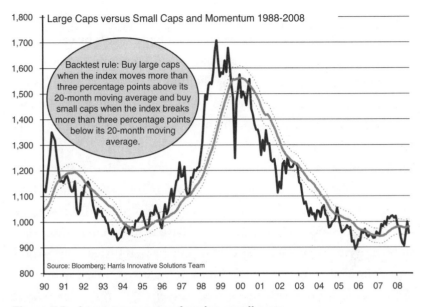

Figure 7.2   Large caps outperforming small caps.

1 percentage point above or below that moving average) would have turned $1,000 into $2,355 over the 20-year period from December 1988 until December 2008. (That calculation assumes that during periods when commodities weren't attractive, he or she had parked that capital in Treasury securities earning a 4% annualized return.) Meanwhile, the buy and hold strategy would have left an investor with only $893 per $1,000 invested (see Figure 7.3).

Moving averages tell us a lot about the direction in which a market index is heading as well as its speed. But a process-driven investor needs more information than that, just as when you see a speeding car on the highway, you want to know whether the driver is trained in high-speed driving, if he or she is intoxicated, how well built the car is, whether it is about to run out of gas, what the weather and highway conditions are, and whether there is something ahead likely to bring the speed demon to an abrupt halt. In the financial markets, the force of a particular move is especially critical. Traders keeping tabs on trading patterns throughout the day will draw conclusions about the durability of a big rally or significance of a large selloff by calculating how many stocks took part in the move and the number of investors who participated, as measured by the trading volume. They'll downplay the significance of a rally, however large, if trading is thin and only a few stocks have driven the index higher. Similarly, they won't panic if a selloff comes the day after the Thanksgiving holiday, when most investors are on vacation. Knowing the breadth of a stock market move—how many stocks or sectors are participating—can tell us more about the inner workings of any big move than just looking at the index's behavior. My Chicago Cubs have managed to put together some impressive winning streaks over their 100-year-long World Series drought and even came within a few games of making it to the World Series for the first time in a century in 2008. But a fan looking beyond those win and loss ratios to the sports world's version of breadth—the skills of their roster of hitters, pitchers, and fielding talent—probably worried how long those streaks could be sustained.

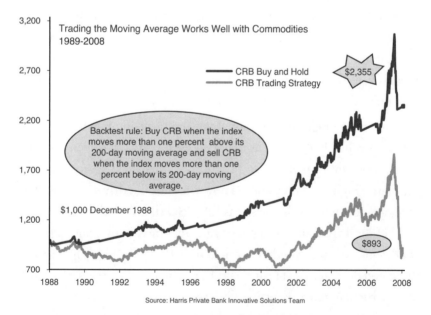

Figure 7.3   Buy and hold versus using the 52-week moving average.

One of the best ways to measure the market's breadth, and thus the strength of any particular trend, is to study the advance/decline line, often referred to as the advance/decline ratio. As its moniker implies, this is simply a way to compare the number of stocks within an index whose prices are climbing, or advancing, and the number whose prices are declining. Although neither I nor any other money manager worth his annual bonus would turn up our noses at a 1% jump in any market index, some 1% gains are more significant than others. Personally, I'd rather have a 1% gain in the Dow to which all index components contribute to one where only 2 of the 30 stocks are sharply higher. An advance/decline ratio can be constructed for any index or for the market as a whole. The broader the participation, the steeper it appears on the chart, and the more bullish the signals that it is sending to technical market analysts. This momentum metric will tell you the degree to which investors are convinced that the trend will last. If you see a jump in the value of a commodity index in which crude oil is heavily weighted—such as the Goldman Sachs Index— you can't assume that it's because of a bull market in commodities. Instead, you need to look beyond the index to see whether crude oil is the only index component that is rising. In that case, you need to ignore the index as an index of the commodity market, pull your cash out of the asset class, and dash for cover. On the other hand, if soybeans, pork bellies, silver, and copper all are participating in the rally to some extent, feel free to celebrate.

To see how this can prove useful in practice, just take a look back to the fall of 2004. A sharp slump left investors worrying that the 2-year-old stock market rally was faltering. From the middle of September to the end of October, the 30 Dow stocks struggled to deal with the possibility of higher interest rates and lower liquidity. On September 14, the Dow closed at 10,318; by October 30, the index had fallen 2.8% to 10,027. Anyone tracking momentum indicators, however, could reassure themselves that the bull market wasn't over. In fact, despite the slide, the advance/decline ratio was sending an upbeat signal; more stocks rose than fell. Sure, watching a slide is never fun, but investors heeding momentum indicators would have been better positioned to resist the temptation to take to booze to drown their sorrows. Indeed, anyone who used the slump as a buying opportunity would have had extra cause for celebration on New Year's Eve. From early November through to the end of 2004, the Dow jumped 11%. That move may have caught skittish emotion-driven investors by surprise, but not those familiar with momentum metrics.

It is sometimes hard for me to understand why so many investors focus only on the surface and fail to look beyond the headlines. I suppose it's a bit like going on a cross-country hike and then encountering a stream or river. It is narrow—I can see the opposite bank easily from where I stand—but the nearest bridge is nowhere in sight. The simplest strategy would be to take off my boots and wade across to the other shore, replace my footwear, and resume my hike. But suppose that instead of a stream, I'm standing in front of a narrow but very deep river, with a strong current? Unprepared, I could be swept off my feet and drown. Similarly, before I jump into the market, I need as much information as I can glean. That information must deal not only with its fundamentals, but the force and conviction lying beneath the surface of any market move. That is what breadth metrics such as the advance/decline ratio can tell you.

Breadth indicators are particularly valuable when the information they provide contradicts what is happening in the market index. At times of maximum bullishness or bearishness, contrarian signals can be hard to detect, much less decipher. This variety, however, is easy to spot and particularly useful. Back in November 1996, for instance, I watched the advance/decline line for the S&P 500 Index start to fall. The fact that more stocks were declining than advancing appeared to suggest that the force of the stock market rally was dissipating. True, many market indicators continued to set record after record over the following years. The Dow Jones Industrial Average, for instance, rocketed to 7,000, then 8,000, and onward to 9,000, with only the occasional blip along the way due to an outside event, such as the emerging markets crisis or the collapse of Long-Term Capital Management in 1998.

But I tried not to be distracted by what the overall Dow index—a relatively small group of only 30 stocks, however important each may be within its own industry—was doing. What preoccupied me was what was happening *within* the larger S&P 500 Index. Because of its size and scope, measuring this benchmark's advance/decline ratio is more meaningful. I found that each upward step by that index, each record broken, occurred with less and less participation. By the end of 1999, only 155 of the 500 companies in the S&P 500 outperformed the index itself, suggesting that investors didn't have much confidence in the future growth prospects of more than two-thirds of S&P stocks. Anyone who spotted that fact might have realized that a bear market was taking shape just offstage. Anyone with an interest in market history would have found the analysis easier still: Back in 1987, when the Dow Jones index reached one new high after another in the months leading up to the crash, the advance/decline ratio was flagging.

Typically, I use breadth indicators as a way to determine whether and when to pull money out of stocks, bonds, or other markets and park it in cash, rather than to tell me about the relative merits of different asset classes. If a market is expensive and running on momentum rather than fundamentals, a deterioration in breadth will often be the best indicator that it's time to jump off the bandwagon. Best of all, it can be applied to any asset class, including commodities. Back in 2000, for instance, the Dow Jones Commodity Index soared 24%, but the number of its 20 components rising in value slipped from 12 to 10. At the very least, those metrics sent commodity investors a mixed message: Yes, the topline results were bullish from a momentum perspective, but bulls needed to at least consider the possibility that momentum was flagging. Those who heeded that message would have been better prepared for the abrupt about-face by the entire index in 2001, when it plunged 22%. I wouldn't say that breadth indicators on their own served as a sell signal, but they certainly were the equivalent of a shot fired across the bow. Outsize volatility of this kind is just one reason commodity investing makes me nervous. Just as in the foreign exchange market, it's hard to establish a "fair" market value for a given commodity. But if you have an overwhelming urge to put your money to work in the world of pork bellies and natural gas, you need to become very comfortable with a wide array of momentum indicators, especially those that provide data on market breadth.

Measuring the market's internal strength in this way will help you understand just how powerful momentum is in any given asset class or sector. Momentum metrics like this also remind you of the need to look beneath the surface. Investors pay a lot of attention to whether stocks are making new 52-week highs. (That is one of those data points that tend to show up in newspaper and online stock charts and to which CNBC anchors like to point.) But how many 52-week highs are there out there, marketwide? And how many other stocks are posting 52-week lows at the same time? That is more useful information. If I see a stock index setting records when a large proportion of its stocks are setting new highs, that reassures me that the market is, indeed, bullish. If the number of 52-week highs and lows is out of whack, however, this metric can also offer an early warning signal.

Norman Fosback, an analyst and editor of *Fosback's Fund Forecaster*, a newsletter based in Boca Raton, Florida, devised a new way to determine when the market is "in gear" (bullish) or "out of gear" (bearish). Whenever his index is rising, that tells him that many stocks are making new highs and new lows at the same time. That tells him that the market's broad trend, as measured by whatever the index is doing, is unreliable, because the performance of its components is all over the map. His reasoning runs as follows: Under normal circumstances, a significant number of stocks post either new highs or new lows. Even if the proportion of stocks making new highs when the market is rising isn't remarkable, that is less crucial than the fact that those that aren't doing so are at least relatively stable. Even if some are unchanged or down slightly, they aren't hitting new lows. To Fosback and his adherents (I'm more of an interested observer, personally) that means that enough stocks are bullish to neutral to be able to conclude there's no serious threat to the market just waiting to strike.

The goal of all these momentum metrics is to help you make macro-level investment decisions, the kind that have the most sweeping impact on your overall returns (as I explained in the first chapter). Using them will also help you make those calls with a greater level of confidence and security. We are all greedy for the maximum possible return. I prefer to earn it with the minimum amount of fear, terror, and risk. If you know how and when to turn to momentum indicators, you can look for early signs of changing market trends. Can paying attention to momentum make a big difference in your returns? Absolutely. Let's say that you were one of the canny investors who, back in early 1990, believed that the recession then underway would end and that technology stocks would prove to be one of the big drivers of long-term investment returns. Assume, for a moment, that your research into market fundamentals drew your attention to the fact that this group was significantly undervalued in both absolute and relative terms. If you acted on that and invested in the Nasdaq 100 Index and held it until the end of 2007, you would have earned $9,797 for every $1,000 you had invested. That translates into an annualized return of about 14.4%, the kind of performance that makes most investors dance for joy.

Of course, you would have taken equally outsize risks to earn those returns—not surprising, when you consider that period includes the worst imaginable 3-year period for technology stocks between 2000 and 2002. That portfolio had an annualized standard deviation of 26.4%, a level of risk high enough to suggest that you were equally likely to have lost your shirt. If you had been able to detect signs that the good times were coming to an end in early 2000, you would have fared still better than you did by holding on through the selloff and the recovery. Had you been able to sell at the peak in March 2000, each $1,000 invested would have earned you a return of $22,244.

Momentum metrics, used correctly, can help you pull your chips off the table at the right time more reliably than any other signals. No, I'm not arguing that you'd all have ended up as billionaires! But anyone who used the signals sent by a 50-day moving average indicator—buying more when the Nasdaq index rose 1 percentage point above the average and then selling when it fell 1 percentage point below the average—over the course of that volatile 17-year period would still have pocketed $10,119 for every $1,000 invested. That's a 14.6% annualized return and one generating a significantly lower standard deviation of 17.2%. In other words, in exchange for paying attention to the signals being sent by our indicator, we get more return *and* the ability to sleep more peacefully at night.

The more contrarian the signal momentum metrics send, the more useful they can be. Let's suppose that our hypothetical investor had decided that using even more momentum metrics would lead, logically, to even more impressive results on an absolute and risk-adjusted basis. Therefore, he decided to hold Nasdaq stocks only when the ratio of new highs to new lows over a 50-day trading period remained positive, on average. There can be too much of a good thing, even momentum indicators, and this is a case in point. That strategy would have caused him to be overly cautious and would have produced an annualized return of only 9.1%, or $4,419 for each $1,000 initially invested. Sure, he would have trimmed his risk level, but only by forfeiting a significant percentage of his potential return. Personally, I don't want to put undue emphasis on any metric that can cause me to be overly cautious and cost my clients money in the shape of foregone returns. So I tend to think of the high-low indicator as a background indicator of sorts, almost as if it were a warning light on my car's dashboard that I heed only when it is blinking. In this case, I wouldn't place too much weight on what this high-low indicator is telling me unless it conflicts with what other momentum metrics are signaling. I value anything that is a contrarian indicator, because that will cause me to double- and triple-check my reasoning.

The momentum factor is one that revolves around what is happening within the markets that I invest in. However, no financial market exists in isolation from the broader world, and often—as we saw dramatically throughout the subprime market meltdown and the ensuing credit crunch and stock market crash—that outside world intrudes dramatically on the markets. That's why I realized the need to study what is happening in that broader context: the economy.

8

The Second Factor: The Economy—Headwind or Tailwind for Stocks?

On a hot day in early September 2007, traders and investors showed up for work early in the morning. They waited, with some trepidation, for the Labor Department's early morning announcement that would tell the world how many new jobs were created or how many jobs had been lost in August. It's a ritual that occurs on the first Friday of every month in the year, but on this day, economists were looking for signs that emerging woes in the real estate industry had spilled over into the labor market. They still expected that overall businesses had managed to add 100,000 or so employees to their collective payroll the previous month. Not so. Instead, when the report was released at 8 a.m., it showed that employers nationwide had actually *cut* a total of 4,000 jobs in the previous month. Even worse, the data for July was revised downward; fewer new jobs had been created that month than the Labor Department had calculated previously. Stock markets from Wall Street to Warsaw plunged; investors from Seattle to Shanghai dashed for shelter.

But why? Why does it matter to your investment plans if the economy starts shedding jobs, as long as your job and those of your friends and family haven't been affected? That's true enough—as far as it goes. But no sensible investor can afford to ignore what is happening in the broader economy. Investors during that long hot summer of 2007 learned the same lessons that generations of their predecessors had learned: that the real or perceived impact of economic events or trends on financial markets and portfolios can be sudden and brutal. The drama of 2008 just reinforced that lesson. Within a week, or even a single trading day, economic news can cause the market to gyrate wildly and leave investors with outsize profits or losses. In the months that have elapsed since then, the lesson has become still more apparent, as the economy moved into a recession.

That is why the second factor you must use in building your investment decision-making process is what is happening in the economy. Understanding momentum will give you insight into what is happening within a given asset class and help you weigh each asset class's relative merits. But you must go further and develop a new set of metrics that will alert you to economic changes that will affect those asset classes. Imagine that you're heading out to sea for a sail down the Atlantic seaboard. You set out from your summer harbor in Rhode Island, bound for Florida. You have been rigorously attentive to the fundamentals. Your boat is seaworthy, all your navigational equipment works accurately, and you've stocked up on all that you'll need for the journey, from food and water to comfortable cushions in the cabin. But setting out to sea without checking the weather would be foolish.

The economy can be just as unpredictable and uncontrollable as the weather. And just as the weather affects our hypothetical sailor's safety, so the economy matters to an investor's financial well-being. The weather may delay a sailor, force a change of route, or perhaps even require the sailor to make repairs to the boat. Economic headwinds can be just as hazardous. An investor caught unprepared might have to postpone retirement, put up with a lower standard of living, or take more risk to compensate for losses. The better prepared you are, the more you can profit from the tailwinds and the better you will be at battling through the storms. Because none of us can control the economy, it's up to us to identify and understand what economic swings are taking place as well as how and when to react to those changes. If you aren't attentive enough to the shifting winds of the economy, your portfolio runs a greater risk of being wrecked on the shoals of a recession or depression.

At any given point in time, the economy functions as a kind of backdrop that favors the growth of one kind of asset class or securities over another. Over long periods of time, what happens in the stock market reflects economic activity. Take a look at Figure 8.1. It shows how quarterly changes in gross domestic product are reflected in the quarterly returns of the S&P 500 Index.

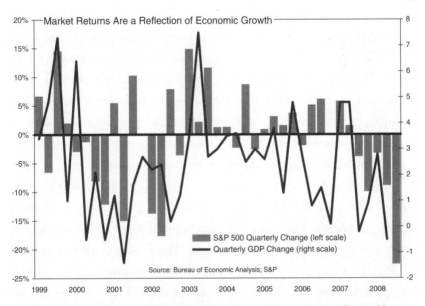

Figure 8.1   Quarterly changes in gross domestic product reflected in quarterly returns of the S&P 500.

Although there can be a lot of "noise" (periods when markets respond to other signals or when investors are distracted or find economic data difficult to read), strong economic growth generally speaking goes hand in hand with above-average stock market returns. Similarly, an economic slump corresponds to a period of sluggish stock market returns or outright losses.

The link is an easy one to understand because it's all about corporate profits. What drives stock prices? The growth (or lack thereof) of profits earned by the companies that issue those stocks. As a general rule, the more profits grow, the higher the company's stock price climbs. When Apple's iPod became a "must-own" for design-conscious hipsters and their imitators, the company's sales and profits soared. The trendy new product had a lot to do with it, but if the economy hadn't been in the midst of a rebound, how many of their customers would have been willing to fork over a few hundred dollars for the wallet-sized device? In a slowing economy, one in which people are losing jobs and trying to scale back their spending, consumer wallets snap shut. The first companies to struggle will be those that sell products or services consumers may view as luxuries (a new iPhone, the safari vacation, the new car, or the pool for the backyard). There is a reason that the county with the highest unemployment rate in early 2009 was dominated by makers of recreational vehicles cutting back on their workforce and production as sales of these luxury goods fell off. Whenever the economy slumps, companies respond by scaling back their own spending, hiring fewer people or purchasing less as they brace for slower sales and lower profits. Other businesses will be more resilient; people will still need to shop at drugstores and buy groceries, although those companies may find sales volumes and margins slide, too. The economy drives profits, which in turn make up a larger part of that economy—12% in 2007, compared to less than 2% in 1947, a reflection of the changes within the private sector as smaller family businesses have given way to larger corporate chains.

Despite its importance, the economy remains just as difficult to forecast as the weather (one reason, perhaps, why the field of economics is sometimes referred to as "the dismal science"). Even in periods of prolonged economic growth, our economy doesn't expand consistently. Spikes and slumps are common, such as those that we all witnessed in the final heady days of the technology boom in 1998 and 1999. Companies nationwide grappled with labor shortages as their employees rushed off to join or form new technology companies.

Companies in "old-economy" industries paid hefty bonuses to anyone who could find a successful candidate for vacant positions. Even high-flying start-ups couldn't find enough bodies to keep up the pace. Veteran economic and business analysts started talking about a new paradigm, a world in which the rules of economic growth involving boom and bust cycles had been revoked.

Sure enough, that boom came to an abrupt and unpleasant end, one that culminated in an economic recession. Happily, investors and economists are sometimes better at anticipating economic transitions. By the time the September 2007 jobs data sparked a stock market selloff, investors and analysts had been fretting about the health of the economy for more than 2 years. Sky-high energy prices worried them, as did the impact of rising interest rates on the real estate market. They were well aware that corporate inventories were rising, while job creation had been slowing as the construction sector laid off employees. Retailers began to report disappointing sales figures.

Few of these twists and turns in the economic cycle surprise me any more. Like most Americans, I've battled through several economic and market downturns during my adult life, as well as enjoying the bursts of prosperity. Back in 1980, when I was doing an internship in Washington, D.C., gasoline shortages meant long lines at gas stations. Worse than that, an emergency law ruled that I could only join those lines on odd-numbered days to fill up the tank of my aging Volkswagen Rabbit. I've grown accustomed to this kind of ebb and flow in the economy, which pundits often refer to as the business cycle. Today, my goal as an investor is to use economic metrics to figure out what stage we are at in that cycle and thus what investments offer the best opportunities. Is the economy in expansion mode, with companies creating new jobs and seeing their sales and profit growth accelerating? Or is that expansion close to peaking, as productive capacity becomes constrained? Perhaps the economy is contracting; business activity is slowing and job losses are starting to rise. The trough is most painful of all, the stage in which the economy hits bottom and the whole world seems bleak. But it's in this stage that the seeds for a new economic expansion are planted.

Each of these four stages suggests investors take a different approach to the financial markets and to the array of available asset classes. When the economy slows, for instance, sectors such as health care are likely to outperform: Those who need to take blood pressure medication will keep buying it as long as they can, even if its price rises. (That's why Colgate Palmolive got away with boosting prices on some of its products in 2008 even as the economy slipped into a recession.) On the other hand, technology stocks tend to be more cyclical. They tend to follow the economic cycle, flourishing when growth is robust and flagging when the economy sours. I can't control where we are in the economic cycle, but I do have the analytical skills to provide us that information and give us clues as to what is on the horizon. You may have a portfolio that is designed to outperform in a strong economy, but if you can't tweak it to reflect the changes after the economy peaks, the outcome will be disastrous. It would be as if someone sneaked into your house while you were out and turned up the temperature of the water in your aquarium. All those tropical fish flourishing because you have been carefully cultivating just the right environment will be transformed into bouillabaisse in an instant.

I began to grasp the way in which the economy and the government's economic policies could play havoc with my best-laid plans in the mid-1980s while living in Boston, in the midst of a frenzied real estate environment. A friend of mine and I decided we would buy some residential housing units, fix them up, and sell them at a hefty profit. We figured that we couldn't lose. We toured a building in what in most markets would have been considered a slum. Still, it was priced at a hefty premium of around $100,000 per unit. We wavered, even as the real estate agent pressed us to sign on the dotted line. Then the Reagan administration suddenly eliminated something called the "accelerated depreciation allowance," a tax break for investing in depreciating assets like real estate. That yanked the rug out from under the real estate market. My friend and I watched the entire Boston-area real estate market pretty much crumble to pieces around us. I put my dreams of becoming a real estate mogul on the shelf and returned to my "day job" managing money with new appreciation for the role in which exogenous events could impact the economy and, in turn, an entire asset class.

Economists love to boil their profession down to lots of numbers. To understand how the economy impacts investments, however, you really need to consider human nature. Trading mortgage-backed securities in the 1980s, I was bemused when homeowners failed to do what seemed very logical to me and renegotiate their mortgages. Their monthly mortgage payments were based on interest rates of 11% or 12%. They could easily refinance at 8% or 9% and save hundreds of dollars a month. What I had failed to factor into my model was the fact that whole segments of the real estate market had been so badly hit by the downturn that owners had no equity left in their houses. No banker in his right mind would lend 120% of the value of a home to a borrower! To refinance, owners would have had to put up more equity, wiping out the benefits of a lower interest rate. (We're seeing a similar phenomenon take shape in 2009, with the added problem—for borrowers—of very stringent credit standards.) It was much better for them to just stay put and keep paying the extra dollars each month and wait for the real estate market to recover some ground, however much havoc that wreaked on my carefully designed models.

The good news? Developing a reliable set of metrics to help you monitor what is happening to the economy is easier than forecasting the weather. And with the right metrics, you have a reasonable chance of steering clear of economic storms or at least minimizing the damage they can do to the portfolio you have carefully assembled based on your analysis of the other four factors. Certainly, most times that I've seen a recession emerge in recent decades, metrics have provided savvy investors with ample warning—and thus with enough time to build protective walls around their portfolio and adjust their holdings accordingly. They also can help you identify those economies (national or regional) that offer the best economic conditions at any given time. Think of the economy as the background or scenery against which all the action of the other four factors is played out.

As is the case with all five factors, however, the key to success is identifying which economic metrics have some kind of predictive power or offer you a tool that will help you weigh your alternatives. There's no such thing as a "good" economy or a "bad" economy, except in the dreams of economists. Rather, the economies of the 200-plus nations in the world are all either more or less attractive than each other at any given point in time. Each of these national economies must grapple with certain harsh realities: The United States, for instance, saw parts of its manufacturing sector vanish first to Mexico, and then more of it head off to China. Most recently of all, ultra-low-wage nations like Cambodia have seized manufacturing market share from both Mexico and China. The 1990s bull market can be seen as a tribute of sorts to our success in coping with that change in our economy, which suddenly was no longer dominated by these manufacturing giants. An influx of new knowledge-based, technology-based, and service-based companies, notably the flurry of new high-technology companies spawned in Silicon Valley, took their place and led the next wave of economic growth. Productivity soared; corporate profitability and personal incomes expanded at an impressive rate. Meanwhile, inflation was kept at bay by the outsourcing of production to low-wage countries: The DVD players and personal computers that American consumers snapped up at lower and lower prices with their higher earning power were made overseas.

But no economy can ever remain frozen at a single point in time. The goal of economic metrics is to figure out at any point in time just where in the cycle the economy is (and at what point others are). Are we emerging? Growing? Peaking? Declining? And what about the other economies in whose securities we could invest as an alternative to those of our home market?

The starting point for an analysis of the economic factors is within our home market. The metrics most helpful to determining what's going on aren't those that grab headlines and drive markets into a frenzy; that kind of data is just too "noisy." The monthly release of figures such as new job creation or retail sales, for instance, tries to measure trends too frequently to be useful, while at the same time sparking too much market volatility to be helpful in an analytical framework. Sure, back in the days when I was trading bonds, I was just as fixated as everyone else still is today on the monthly jobs number on the first Friday of every month. But as I grew to realize that the fewer trades I made and the more those were based on longer-term indicators that measured the bigger picture, the better I performed. I understood I needed to steer clear of all the fuss surrounding those monthly data points. (After all, even if I correctly predicted the number right, I could still take a big hit if investors responded in a way that I hadn't predicted or thought would be irrational—a not infrequent occurrence.)

Other pieces of economic data can be useful only selectively. Some traders jump on retail sales data as a signal of how the economy is faring, arguing that because consumer spending makes up such a big chunk of the U.S. economy, the willingness of consumers to fork over spare cash at their local Wal-Mart is a useful indicator of the economy's health. Well, not really. Leaving aside all the problems inherent in measuring retail spending, it is really only helpful when it comes to telling me what is happening to a handful of big retailers. I've already demonstrated to you early on in this book that investors capture the biggest bang for their bucks making asset-allocation decisions. So, you and I need data that tells us about the health of the economy as a whole. Because retailing is only one of several sectors in the S&P 500 Index, and far from the largest, even a reliable retail sales figure won't significantly hint as to what is likely to affect the overall stock market. (The one exception, in this case, is if I have, or want to include, commercial real estate as an asset class in my portfolio. In that case, I want to know what's happening to sales of the companies leasing that property, retailers among them.)

Traders and other market pundits track inflation data, such as the producer price index or the consumer price index, but that might be less useful than it seems. It may indicate whether inflation is on the rise or ebbing. So far, so good. But it doesn't help me understand whether the stock market will thrive. The stock market is made up of sectors that respond in very different ways to inflation: Even expectations of higher inflation are toxic to utility stocks and damage the financial sector, as rising interest rates eat into profits and make their returns less competitive. Technology stocks, meanwhile, historically thrive when prices are climbing.

Above all, these well-known and widely tracked economic indicators share a single large flaw: They are backward looking. They tell us what has happened in the recent past. (Indeed, the more useful they are, the more firmly rooted in the past they are: I find jobs data and retail sales data that summarize the trend of the past 12 months to be more useful than a single data point about the events of the past few weeks.) As investors who want to make rational asset-allocation decisions, we don't need to know what *has* happened but rather what is likely *to* happen. What is more useful, being warned by your television meteorologist that a blizzard is on its way, or watching footage of snow-removal crews struggling to clear the streets? The latter might be more entertaining, but odds are it will be less helpful. Similarly, the metrics I seek out are those that can tell me whether the economic environment is positive, negative, or neutral; whether it's likely to encourage a growth in profits and thus a bull market for stocks or is more likely to favor bonds.

I find the metrics that help me answer that question are those tied to interest rates (specifically in metrics tied to the yields on bonds, because the bond market is the most direct reflection of the investment "backdrop" that I have found). Every slight change in economic trends, in inflation expectations or in credit risk is reflected (and sometimes magnified) in the market for Treasury bills, notes, and bonds. What happens to the prices and yields (the amount of interest paid to investors as a function of the prevailing price) on these securities embodies a whole array of investor expectations. Worried that corporate profits are declining? Odds are that if the market shares your unease, there will be a flight to "quality" in the shape of Treasury securities, whose prices will rise, and yields will fall as a result. At the same time, the gap between the yield on a Treasury note or bond and that on a corporate bond may widen—investors feel safer owning the government-backed security than they do taking the risk that the corporate issuer will buck the trend and earn enough in profits to maintain its regular interest payments to bondholders. If you want a snapshot of investor expectations of the economy, of corporate profits, of the relative risks of stocks and bonds, all you need to do is look at bond market data. Are the spreads on bond yields issued by low-credit-quality companies and those issued by companies with investment-grade ratings narrower than has been the case historically? That can tell you whether the economy is contracting or expanding and give you insight into lenders' and investors' respective attitudes to risk, confidence, and speculation.

For me, the crucial economic metrics, the ones that tell me whether it's time to shun or embrace U.S. stocks, are the shapes of two different curves. One is the yield curve, calculated by plotting the yields of an array of Treasury securities of different maturities, from 30 days to 30 years. The second is the "federal funds" futures curve, established by plotting the yield associated with futures contracts tied to whether investors expect Federal Reserve monetary policy makers to raise or lower key lending rates. (That might sound complicated, but really it isn't: Buyers and sellers of the publicly traded futures contracts essentially agree on where they think Fed interest rates will be at various dates in the future; the curve takes shape when these are all plotted out.) It's not the absolute levels of the yields or expected interest rates that are important, but the shape of the curves themselves.

Let's start by looking at the yield curve (see Figure 8.2). Traditionally, this slopes upward from left to right. The further away the date on which the bond matures, the higher the yield. That reflects the fact that lenders view the risk and uncertainty of lending as growing as the repayment date stretches further into the future.

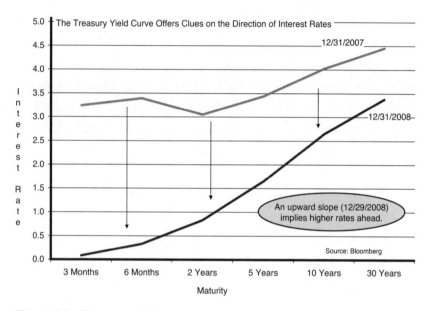

Figure 8.2   Treasury yield curve.

If the U.S. Treasury wants to borrow money for 10 years, it will have to pay more in annual interest than it would have if it wanted the cash for 30 days; more can go wrong in 10 years than 30 days. When the yield curve takes this kind of positive slope—and where there is a gap between the yield on the 3-month Treasury bill and the 10-year Treasury note of more than 2 percentage points—that yield spread tells me that the economic backdrop is generally bullish for stocks. A steep yield curve (one where the slope goes up dramatically) signals strong economic growth. That is potentially a great stock market environment so long as the growth doesn't get to the point where inflationary pressures tempt Federal Reserve monetary policy authorities to get into the act and choke it off by raising interest rates.

One of the best predictors of the economy's health that I have been able to find is the spread (over the past 50 years) between the 3-month Treasury bills and the 10-year Treasury notes. When that yield curve inverts—that is, when the yields investors can earn on 10-year Treasurys are *lower* than those on shorter-term securities—the yield curve is telling me that investors expect an economic slowdown, even though this might not yet be showing up in the data being released on a monthly or quarterly basis. But it tells me that it's time to consider pulling back from the U.S. stock market and look at other asset classes in search of alternatives that offer more upside potential or even a better chance of maintaining their value. Over the past quarter century, the yield curve has been inverted only 8% of the time; in many cases, these inversions were followed by either an economic slowdown or an outright recession.

So how can you, as an investor, look at the yield curve and get a useful signal? One of the best things to do is to track what happens to the yields on both the 2-year and 10-year Treasury notes. If the latter is higher than the 2-year yield, the economy is expanding. If the 10-year yield is lower than the 2-year yield, it's an economic contraction: Bond investors are betting that interest rates will fall in the coming months and years. Because the stock market thrives in an expansion and suffers in a contraction, you probably won't be startled to learn that over the past 30 years the average monthly return of the Dow Jones Industrial Average when the 10-year yield exceeds that on the 2-year notes is about 1%, compared to 0.2% when the yield curve is inverted and the 2-year yield exceeds that on the 10-year Treasury note. The yield curve's shape is an even more dramatic predictor of stock market performance looking a year out (our target time horizon). When the yield curve is positive (that is, when the yield on the 10-year Treasury note exceeds that on the 2-year note), the Dow Jones Industrial Average has returned an average of 11.4% over the following 12 months. An inverted yield curve? The 30 stocks in the Dow benchmark returned less than half of that (an average of only 5.2%) in the following 12-month period.

One of the risks associated with an economic expansion is that the expansion will overheat and turn into inflation. In emerging markets such as China and India, growth rates of 6%, 7%, or even 10% can be tolerated and even welcomed. In more-developed economies, however, that tends to create inflationary bubbles that, if not slowly deflated by monetary policy makers, can explode with ugly consequences, as those of us who struggled through the 1970s can remember all-too vividly. All things being equal, the Fed prefers to see what economists refer to as a "soft landing"—a period of expansion followed by a gentle contraction—to a "hard landing" of the kind that produces a recession. That's why Fed policy makers jump into action whenever they perceive the economic expansion to be too dramatic. And that's why I also keep a keen eye on the shape of the federal funds futures curve, which signals the market's collective thinking about what the Fed's interest rate policy is likely to be into the future. The steeper that curve, the greater the likelihood that interest rates will be higher in the future, creating a headwind that companies must confront. A flat to inverted yield curve suggests that the Fed is more likely to lower key lending rates, and that the business environment is benign; that policy makers are more likely to encourage companies to borrow money to grow their businesses than they are to install artificial roadblocks to higher profits in the shape of higher interest rates.

These two indicators are a starting point for evaluating the economic environment in which I make asset-allocation decisions. Used alone, they can offer the single most valuable clues to the direction in which the economy is headed. They give me a capsule summary. If I have the time, interest, and inclination, I can venture further afield in search of confirmation or additional, more-specialized indicators. For instance, the Conference Board's Composite Index of Leading Indicators is another forward-looking gauge of economic well-being. It tracks ten components, ranging from the number of new building permits issued to the average number of hours worked weekly in the manufacturing sector (and including the yield differential between the 10-year

Treasury note and the Federal funds rate) and wraps them up in one neat package. It's not as reliable a predictor as the shape of the yield curve has proved to be over the past 30 years, however. Still, I have discovered that when the rate of change in that index hovers above 0.1 for 3 months in a row, the economic outlook seems positive, and the Dow Jones Industrial Average returns an average of 10.9% in the following 12 months. On the other hand, if the rate of change in the index falls below 0.1 for 3 consecutive months, there is a negative trend in place, and the Dow's average 12-month return following that falls to 9.7%.

These days, the kind of asset-allocation decision I make in response to economic metrics is no longer likely to be just a simple switch from stocks into bonds. Indeed, faced with a negative environment for U.S. stocks, my own first choice isn't to pull my money out and invest in the bond market instead. These days, Treasury notes are an expensive luxury investment rather than being attractive in their own right, because the Treasury is printing money at a rapid rate as part of its efforts to stabilize the banking and financial system. (Eventually, the value will drop and inflation will pick up; holders of these Treasury securities will be left holding the bag.) So, if the economic backdrop looks as if it will be bearish for, say, U.S. growth stocks, my next step is to ask whether the same holds true for value stocks. Or if the rapid growth rates, which tend to favor small-cap stocks, have abated, do I believe that the economy has enough upside potential to make larger-cap stocks attractive? What's bad for one part of the stock market can be good news for another kind of equity. For instance, the weakness in the U.S. dollar that sent the greenback to the lowest level in decades against other major world currencies in the first few months of 2008 was good news for investors in overseas stocks. Even if those stocks turned in relatively lackluster returns in absolute terms, when translated from the euro, the pound, or the Canadian dollar back into U.S. dollars, the actual profits from owning the stock were much larger for a U.S. investor. For the same reason, a slump in the greenback also tends to favor large U.S. multinational companies, which earn an outsize portion of their sales from overseas markets. Small-cap stocks, which tend to be net importers rather than exporters, would be at a relative disadvantage. That is just the kind of disparity in potential market returns that can boost the investment returns for those who spot it early on.

Watching economic metrics means monitoring global data, not just that produced by our domestic economy. After all, investment opportunities exist globally, and thanks to the interrelationship between trading partners, what happens in another country's economy can affect our own. As a broad rule of thumb, I argue that any stock portfolio should consider having a third of its capital invested outside the United States. Our stock market now makes up only slightly more than half of the world's total stock market capitalization. So if the business cycle in the United States has peaked and is beginning to contract, that doesn't automatically signal that you should bolt for the low-yielding bond market. Rather, the logical next step is to look abroad in search of a region where the economy is expanding, as measured by its general business activity (such as growth in corporate profits) and gross domestic product. Despite the fact that economies worldwide can be interrelated, great disparities remain in both the direction and rate of economic (and market) growth. Japan, for instance, has been a longstanding laggard, with hints of economic turnarounds and market recoveries to date having proved so far to be nothing more than false dawns. In contrast, China's runaway growth and market expansion (in terms of the number and nature of the stocks listed on the various exchanges) has offered immense opportunity, along with outsize volatility and risk. Again, the trick is to find the most attractive economic backdrop on a *relative* basis, adjusting for the different level of risk you take on whenever you leave your domestic market.

There are headaches that go along with applying the economic factor to our global investment decisions. Just because the economy of one country or region is beginning to wane doesn't mean another is poised to thrive, for instance. The majority of economic downturns flow from local excesses, just as the dot.com boom in the United States produced the recession that finally ended in 2002. But that kind of downturn in the United States is certainly felt by our trading partners, although its impact can often be more muted than some fear mongers, buzzing anxiously about "contagion," believe. Today, as American consumers try to repair their personal balance sheets, the ramifications are clearly global, although most of the pain will be felt here at home. Typically, problems with a domestic market produce a situation where stocks overseas are *relatively* more attractive, even if the correlation isn't perfect in terms of timing or magnitude.

Another mostly local economic condition is inflation. Just because the prices of consumer or business goods are growing rapidly in one economy doesn't mean that the same is true throughout the global economy. China, for instance, is exporting its growth to neighbors and trading partners, but it hasn't exported much inflation despite average GDP growth of 10% a year over the past decade. An inflationary economy will see its bond investments decline in value, but bonds issued in economies that are experiencing relatively lower inflation rates will continue to thrive, history suggests. Keeping tabs on local conditions such as inflation and consumer spending is particularly critical for an investor who is interested in capturing some of the outsize growth that can come from investing in the rapidly expanding economies in emerging markets such as China, India, and Brazil. It isn't just U.S. demand for Chinese goods that has fueled Chinese growth; the swing factor is the surge in demand from local consumers, particularly an emerging middle class that may already outnumber the entire population of North America. Now that the valuations applied to these emerging markets have reached levels that approximate those of the S&P 500, tracking those bits and pieces of economic data that give us clues to relative strengths and weaknesses is becoming more important, because they might well provide the first signal that a change in other factors, particularly fundamentals, is on its way.

Compared to other metrics, the tools investors use in evaluating the economic climate might seem more like blunt implements than surgically precise instruments. That's just fine. When it comes to the economy, what you need can be found without having to sort through and fine-tune each set of economic data. The economy, like a giant oil tanker, changes direction only slowly and after giving lots of warning. If you're watching the right indicators—the yield curves that spell out forward direction rather than metrics that tell you where you have already been—you'll get enough advance notice of a change in direction to begin planning changes in your investment portfolio. Precision is less important than accuracy in predicting the general direction and approximate time frame. The objective is to be able to dig just deeply enough into the vast amount of economic data that exists to be able to get a valid and reliable signal of the stock market's health: thumbs up or thumbs down.

9

The Third Factor: Liquidity—
Follow the Money

If you don't have it, you can't spend it.

That's one of those life lessons that all of us learn at some point along the way, together with the ugly inevitability of death and taxes. Money is a finite commodity, and all of us must consider that whenever we make our spending decisions. In other words, before plunking down the cash for that Hawaiian vacation, you need to consider your liquidity position. Do you have that money available to spend? If you spend it on that vacation, what will you *not* be able to spend it on? Will you be able to replace that cash through fresh earnings and, if so, how quickly?

These are just some of the questions that a discussion of liquidity sparks at the personal level. From our earliest years, we all begin to be aware of how available money is—how easily it can be acquired— and the need to make spending decisions. When you're a child, how much cash you have in your pockets (your liquidity position) depends largely on your parents. When my two daughters, Elise and Emily, were young enough to be entirely dependent on us for their cash flow, we lived in Florida. Every weekend, we could head for one of the state's seemingly endless array of theme parks in which the girls could run amok. Being able to take our children on fantasy vacations on a regular basis was wonderful, but I dreaded certain aspects of each such excursion, particularly the mandatory trip to the souvenir shops. The endless array of plastic, nylon, and plush trinkets was daunting and so, too, was the clamor of our daughters for one after another of these objects. My wife and I knew that we would never be able to persuade either girl to just walk away from this junk. Instead, we used liquidity considerations as a way to instill reasonable behavior. We'd capitulate, but intelligently, by giving each girl $20 to spend each day as she wished. She could fritter it away or save both days' allowances to make one big $40 purchase. This liquidity-based approach transformed our daughters into discriminating comparison shoppers. Faced with a finite amount of capital, they still spent it all; what else could be expected? Elise, at the age of eight, was the more aggressive spender; the $20 disappeared the day it was dispensed, and she would sometimes plead for an advance on the second day's allowance. But Emily, then age four, hung on to her capital until the end of the second day for a single shopping spree.

What, you ask, does this have to do with liquidity? The degree to which our girls had money in their pockets depended on our access to capital as well as our willingness to finance their shopping excursions. With their $20 a day, Elise and Emily could then decide whether to contribute their dollars to the theme park's revenues, boosting its own liquidity. In fact, our weekend adventures served as examples of the two major kinds of liquidity: funding liquidity (our willingness to make capital available; to serve as our daughters' bankers) and market liquidity (our daughters' ability to easily spend that capital on miscellaneous stuffed animals).

Liquidity is the third factor in my model because without it financial markets and even economies cease to function efficiently. Someone out there—a central bank, an employer, a parent, or an elderly aunt writing a will—serves as a provider of liquidity, and the endless to-and-fro sloshing of liquidity from one part of the economy to another ends up powering the economy and financial markets.

The best illustration of liquidity's importance I have ever heard came from a friend of mine, Jane Esser, who once told me to think of liquidity as if it were gasoline, and companies as automobiles. "It doesn't matter if you run a Bentley or a Yugo, without liquidity, you'll grind to a halt." What's true for automobiles is the same for corporate America. The deeper the pool of liquidity and the more accessible it is, the easier it is for economic growth to occur and for stock prices to gain ground. When liquidity becomes less abundant, the economy and markets alike become more subject to retreats of various degrees of magnitude. The troubles of insurance giant American International Group (AIG), for instance, can be traced to a lack of liquidity (the firm's inability to sell its assets at anything approaching their true value). The value of its assets exceeded that of its liabilities, but in the absence of a market for those assets—in an absence of liquidity—that didn't matter. The 2008 government bailout of AIG became inevitable because the liquidity that is available in most conditions and is required to operate simply evaporated.

Essentially, liquidity is a gauge of how much money is flowing through all parts of the financial system. And just as happens at Disney World, when there is cash around, spending and investment often follow. At first glance, it seems foolish for luxury retailers to open large boutiques in Las Vegas. After all, don't casinos win all the time at the expense of their customers? So why would visitors spend their money in these retail outlets? But the realities of liquidity triumph. There are some winners in Las Vegas. And there is lots of liquidity, generated both by those winners and by losers, who come to Las Vegas with lots of cash and are quite willing to squander what cash they haven't already lost to the slot machines on a new handbag or a high-end watch. Las Vegas is a temple to the gods of liquidity.

When liquidity evaporates, as we witnessed throughout the autumn of 2008, any securities market can turn sour very quickly. Traders worriedly scour a slow-moving market in search for signs that a "buyer's strike" may be in the offing. In this worst-case scenario, buyers vanish altogether, either because they don't have access to capital to invest or spend or because they are too fearful to put that capital to work. (In 2008, the culprit was counterparty credit risk, aggravated by the bankruptcy filing of Lehman Brothers; banks were afraid to lend to one another for fear that the borrower would collapse with the loan still outstanding.) Indeed, there's an important link between investor psychology and liquidity across the entire economy. When money is available to us—when our salaries rise, when we get a bonus—we are more likely to invest or spend. And when we feel our jobs might be at risk, or that we may need our spare cash for medical bills, for instance, we pull back. We start shopping at Target rather than at Saks Fifth Avenue.

Keeping an eye on liquidity metrics can alert us to problems and opportunities. In early 2008, suspecting liquidity would be an ongoing issue for the financial markets, I built a liquidity "dashboard" to measure how easily companies could access new capital should they need it. One key metric it involves is the value of the Japanese yen. Because hedge funds tended to borrow money by shorting yen, a rise in the yen's value would tell me that hedge fund borrowing was falling. I also looked at credit spread changes, because widening spreads would warn me that lenders were becoming more cautious. I added metrics dealing with stock and bond market volatility to round out my dashboard, so that if liquidity deteriorated, a whole host of warning lights should start to flash. With my new metrics-driven tool, I could monitor liquidity levels on a daily basis, the same way a meteorologist tracks changes in weather conditions. By February 2008, liquidity had begun to dry up, market volatility was spiking, and credit spreads widened. Still, the yen's value remained little changed, suggesting that hedge funds, at least, still had ample funds. Then in September, the yen abruptly spiked, signaling trouble in the hedge fund world. Suddenly, those leveraged players no longer had access to the credit on which their investment strategies depended, and many were forced to put entire portfolios up for sale at whatever prices they could obtain. Clearly, liquidity played a significant role in leading to—and signaling—the gargantuan selloffs in stock and bond markets that began that month.

As investors, we need to ask ourselves about the state of liquidity just as we want to know about what is happening in the economy and to become aware of any changes on your side or outlook for the stock market. Is the liquidity trend on your side, or are you trying to fight the trend? That's the question you need to ask, and metrics that help you address it collectively represent the third factor. In evaluating liquidity, you need to know whether the liquidity trend is in your favor. The degree to which money is readily available and investors are prepared to allocate it to the market isn't a primary driver of stock market returns over the medium to long term, especially when compared to factors such as the economy or fundamentals. But, in the absence of liquidity, defined as a steady inflow of new capital into the stock market, it's hard for a rally to endure.

Even novice traders try to monitor the extent to which a market advance is "confirmed," as trading desk jargon puts it, by the number of trades that contribute to that move. Market veterans are prone to view an outsize move in the Dow Jones Industrial Average or other index— say, a 350-point move rise in the Dow benchmark—that takes place amid thin trading as less bullish than a smaller one of only 150 points or so in the midst of a lot of buying. The latter, they know, signals a greater degree of conviction and thus a greater likelihood that the move will prove lasting. I'm not talking about a 1-day event when a group of hedge fund managers are sideswiped by a poor earnings report. Their selling is likely to be met within a day or two by bargain hunting by longer-term investors and normal tight spreads between prices bid and offered for the stock are likely to return quickly. Rather, I'm thinking of what happens when those buyers fail to show up on the day after a selloff (when the only people eager to trade all want to sell). That is the kind of market investors like myself struggled through in October 2008, when, for eight ugly sessions in a row, the Dow average slumped as much as 700 or 800 points, each day, every day. That kind of market, left unchecked, can turn into a death spiral as poor liquidity damages both prices and investor confidence, which in turn further damages liquidity.

Liquidity comes into play at all levels of the financial markets. Individual securities have their own liquidity dynamics, and so do industry sectors and asset classes. In a perfectly liquid market, there are so many buyers and sellers that any transaction, regardless of whether it is a purchase or a sale, can be executed without having to offer a market value discount to facilitate a quick sale. Over short periods, a lack of liquidity means there are fewer buyers than sellers, and the same is true in reverse, creating artificial demand and, if left unchecked, a bubble. When AIG fell victim to a lack of liquidity, it was because it couldn't sell assets at their "true" worth because there were no buyers with capital to transact business and therefore the firm couldn't realize the value of those assets. The higher up the food chain liquidity becomes an issue for the market, the bigger problem (or opportunity) it becomes, and the greater the number of investors affected. If the liquidity in a single stock evaporates, that will hurt only that stock's owners. As the credit crunch of 2007 and 2008 showed, however, the lack of liquidity across global credit markets affected everyone from the smallest individual investor up to and including powerful central banks and their governments. Indeed, the latter took unprecedented measures in repeated efforts to inject liquidity into the markets and stave off complete paralysis in the credit markets and an economic recession. In some ways, the Federal Reserve serves the role of parents of importunate children at amusement parks: They are the lender of last resort, when there is no liquidity forthcoming anywhere else. And when even the Fed can't work its magic, as happened in October 2008, it's up to the government itself to step in and restore order by getting capital flowing again, even when that comes with a $700 billion price tag.

Keeping an eye on liquidity can help us distinguish between market slumps that are really buying opportunities and those that are signs of serious economic problems. In the market retreats of the autumn of 1998 and the autumn of 2000, stock prices were falling, and the spreads on corporate bonds were widening, signaling that investors were becoming more averse to taking market risks. But analysts who paid attention to the market demands for credit and money could detect a difference between the two periods. In the final months of 2000, liquidity was sluggish, these pundits concluded. They reached that decision after looking at the growth in money supply, or M2 as it's known on Wall Street, a figure that represents all cash-like balances held in everything from savings and checking accounts to bank-issued CDs. In 1998, M2 was still robust. Financial markets, flush with cash, rebounded, and the stock market rally resumed. In contrast, the slump in liquidity in late 2000 did presage a bear market that lasted 3 years.

I have found that it's possible to monitor a wide array of liquidity-related metrics, starting at the very top with the amount of money the Federal Reserve itself is prepared to allow all the players in the economy to have at their disposal. (Think of this as the central bank's equivalent of each of my daughters to spend, say, combined with how much we spent on ride tickets and food items, along with the spending of the thousands of other parents in each theme park that day.) One of the first questions to ask is whether the Fed and other lenders throughout the financial system are making it easy or difficult for us to borrow. The easier it is to obtain money, the greater the liquidity and the greater the potential for some of that capital to flow into the stock market. Low interest rates are one signal that can mean borrowing is "easy" and that credit is widely available. It's a bit more complicated in practice because borrowers have different credit ratings, borrowing needs, and time horizons, while lenders have different cash reserves and lending criteria. Just because the interest rate on a Treasury security happens to be low doesn't mean that liquidity is plentiful.

To understand how the liquidity process works, I'll show you how the interest rate of a 10-year bond issued by a corporation is typically calculated. The first question is how much return lenders are demanding in exchange for tying up their capital for 10 years. A good basis for comparison is the yield of inflation-protected Treasury notes—the closest thing that there is to a risk-free return, insulated from the impact of inflation over that period. In early 2008, that

10-year "real" rate was 1.47%, signaling that the Treasury would pay that amount annually to individuals or institutions willing to buy these securities. That's at the low end; yields on these securities have ranged from as high as 4.33% to as little as 1.28%, and averaged 2.78%. But a corporate lender (a bank) needs to be compensated for the potential impact of inflation on their returns (for any erosion in the purchasing power of their capital while it is in the hands of the borrower). Therefore, both borrower and lender have to agree on what kind of inflation is likely, and then adjust the interest rate upward accordingly. In early 2008, when the inflation-protected Treasury note yielded 1.47%, the yield on the 10-year fixed-rate Treasury note was 3.77%: The difference, 2.3 percentage points, represents that inflation premium.

Of course, lending to the corporate world involves more risk than lending to the U.S. Treasury! Even General Electric, although it carries the same triple-A rating (although the company has since been downgraded) from credit rating agencies as does the Treasury, is seen by lenders as a bigger credit risk. So, just as they want to be compensated for inflation risk, lenders want a few extra percentage points in yield in exchange for that additional credit risk. This difference, known as the *credit spread*, varies immensely depending on the category of issuer, the economic conditions and outlook, and the general liquidity environment. If Moody's Investor Service concludes that ACME Widget Co. is a poor credit risk, ACME's borrowing costs will soar, and the credit spread will widen. Or if XYZ Retailers reports higher earnings tomorrow, their credit spread may narrow as lenders believe the risk that they won't be repaid has fallen. As of this writing, an issuer with a triple-B credit rating from one of the agencies can be expected to pay a relatively high rate, 2.51 percentage points above what the Treasury would have to pay in exchange for a 10-year loan. In tough economic times, investors tend to require a higher yield to lend to lower-quality borrowers.

Other factors are also at work. If a company's bonds aren't very easy to trade—either because there aren't many around or because they appeal to relatively few investors—lenders will demand a further premium to compensate for that lack of secondary market liquidity. (This is often seen in the private placement market, for instance, where securities rarely change hands.) Pricing can be further complicated by any special terms or provisions associated with the loan. For instance, if a company wants to be able to buy back its bonds later to reduce its interest expenses, the cost of that "call option" may be another percentage point or two in yield. After all, if the option is exercised, the lender would then have the hassle of having to reinvest their capital. (Borrowers do try to buy back or refinance debt if interest rates fall or their cash position or needs change dramatically.)

So rather than interest rates, yield spreads turn out to be the metric that is most useful in understanding liquidity in the financial system. For instance, if you are interested in what is happening to industrial companies, you can measure the current yield on bonds issued by industrial firms with similar credit ratings and features to those issued by the Treasury. Then compare that yield spread to the historical yield spread for that group. When the only thing that is different is the time period (today, compared to 6 months or a year ago), you can tell whether capital has become more available or more scarce for the sector depending on whether spreads have narrowed or widened. That will tell you a lot about how willing lenders are to take different kinds of risks, and how much liquidity is truly present in different parts of the market.

Analyzing the finer points of credit spreads is one of those pastimes that bond geeks adore but individual investors tire of quickly. So let's move to the other end of the liquidity spectrum, where it is possible to identify and track a different array of liquidity-related metrics based on money flows. Analyzing this data can help us understand the extent to which liquidity is ample or scarce, and thus whether this factor is likely to boost or impede a particular asset class's future performance. These metrics can also help us identify areas in which liquidity levels are changing. One of the best-known examples of money flow metrics are mutual fund flows. This data, reported weekly or monthly by specialist groups, shows how much investors are allocating to certain kinds of mutual fund (inflows), how much others are withdrawing (outflows), and the net impact, whether positive or negative. The theory is that over time, tracking flows will give you a broad picture of liquidity in the shape of the number of dollars flowing into (or out of) mutual fund coffers. You can also drill down more narrowly and see what is happening within key sectors such as technology stocks, where a significant number of dedicated technology funds exist. Some pundits called the outsize returns provided by the volatile Chinese stock market between 2005 and 2007 a triumph of liquidity over fundamentals; investors, carried away by the excitement surrounding the prospect of betting on the future spending of 1.3 billion Chinese citizens, threw money into China-themed stocks and funds at a frenzied pace even as valuations soared.

I find the most useful mutual fund flows data comes from the world of closed-end mutual funds. As I've already explained, whenever a new investor appears on the horizon at an open-end fund, the fund company simply creates new shares in the fund to sell to him or her and then invests the new cash alongside that of existing investors. But when a new investor wants to buy shares of a closed-end fund, he or she has to buy shares of the fund from a willing seller. If there is a greater demand for the shares of, say, large-cap value stock closed-end funds than there is a supply of existing investors prepared to sell at the prevailing price, that price will rise and may even exceed the net asset value of the fund. That may seem illogical—why should people be willing to pay more for a collection of stocks that they could buy more cheaply elsewhere? But it does happen in the world of closed-end mutual funds, whenever an individual manager, fund, or asset class becomes so compelling that investors bet on future potential rather than current values. Liquidity takes over. Similarly, if there aren't enough willing buyers to snap up shares in the closed-end fund, the stock price can fall to a discount to its net asset value.

Monitoring these closed-end fund premiums and discounts offers an insight into liquidity trends, particularly investors' appetite for certain asset classes at varying times and in varying circumstances. For instance, the Nuveen Real Estate Income Fund (a closed-end fund), which trades on the American Stock Exchange under the symbol JRS, traded at a hefty discount to its net asset value when compared to its average over time. (The fund was launched in November 2001.) But beginning in February 2006, the fund's average discount to net asset value began to shrink. By that August, it was trading at a small premium for the first time since 2002. The move suggested that the fund and its asset class were both becoming more popular. Not surprisingly, the fund's premium to net asset value peaked in December 2006, the same month that the market for real estate investment trusts as a group peaked ahead of the downturn in the real estate market that lay ahead the following year.

Big liquidity changes can be particularly visible and important in smaller markets like real estate investment trusts (REITs). Even after massive inflows in 2006, the global REIT market had only $764 billion in assets, according to Ernst & Young. Consider the Dow Jones REIT exchange-traded fund (or ETF), which is listed under the symbol IYR. This fund is one of the most popular vehicles among investors interested in gaining exposure to publicly traded REITs. In contrast to closed-end funds and like mutual funds, the architects of ETFs simply create more shares to accommodate new investors and retire shares to satisfy redemptions. Therefore, tracking the number of shares outstanding of any ETF over time gives us some insight of the amount of liquidity flowing into its asset class. In the case of the REIT market, IYR is a great proxy for liquidity. The fund was launched in June 2000 with 300,000 shares. Within a week, that number had nearly doubled to hit 500,000. By December 2006, the last year in which the sector saw strong returns, the number of shares of IYR outstanding had multiplied *44-fold* (see Figure 9.1). For every year of its existence, the number of IYR shares had increased at an astounding annualized rate of 90%. When you see liquidity grow at that kind of dramatic pace—especially when the growth is associated with a relatively small asset class—you shouldn't ignore it. Indeed, anyone who followed liquidity and invested in REITs for that 6-year period did very well. Of course, liquidity can be less reliable as an indicator when analyzing larger asset classes or even large sectors, because the impact of a determined amount of inflow (or outflow) will always have a smaller impact on larger pools of capital.

Figure 9.1   Dow Jones REIT exchange-traded fund.

Of all the different kinds of liquidity that investors can monitor, perhaps most crucial of all is what I call "big liquidity." This is the kind of liquidity controlled by central bankers such as Alan Greenspan, Ben Bernanke, and their peers at the Bank of Canada, the European Central Bank, the Bank of England, and other major central banks. When individuals turn our own personal spigots—when we collect our bonuses and spend or invest them, when we open up a new line of credit, when we give money to our children to spend in theme parks—we give liquidity a small boost. But unless vast numbers of us act in roughly the same way at roughly the same time, there is no way that we can approach the impact of a central bank's decision on a macro basis to make liquidity more available to all of us. In normal times, central bankers perform a kind of monitoring service: They evaluate liquidity levels elsewhere in the financial system. Do banks have enough cash on their balance sheets, and are they willing to make that available to qualified borrowers? What other pools of capital can an investor draw on? If other sources of liquidity vanish (as happened throughout the credit crunch), it falls to the central bankers to open the spigot to allow new cash flow into the market and, hopefully, fuel the market. As we all saw in 2007 and 2008, that can be accomplished in a straightforward manner, by lowering interest rates, or through more complex maneuvers that put more capital in the hands of commercial lenders and give them incentives to send that money out into the hands of borrowers.

A first step in monitoring "big liquidity" is keeping an eye on what's happening with M2—that measurement of money supply growth that conveniently tracks how much cash-like assets all of us collectively possess, which is calculated and disclosed monthly by the Federal Reserve. When M2 surges, that's good news for stock market returns. The degree to which the economy can grow—a critical ingredient in stock market performance, as I discussed in the preceding chapter—depends on the rate of growth in money supply. If money supply grows faster than inflation, that's bullish for stocks because money is becoming more abundant. All things being equal, more money available means more money that is borrowed or given and more money spent. Still, if production grows faster than money supply over long periods of time, that can have a downside. As money becomes scarce, the cost of borrowing rises, the economy slows, and spending falters. It's a bit like a coal-fired steam engine. As long as the fireman shoveling coal into the boiler can do so with just the right amount of coal on his shovel and at just the right speed, the engine chugs along at just the right pace. Too much steam, too little coal, or an exhausted fireman unable to keep up the pace—all alter the picture; the train slows down or the boiler overheats.

In normal times, the central bankers serve more as monitors of liquidity than as actors. When they do decide to inject new liquidity, they must gauge how much capital is needed to jump-start the financial markets, and determine when the liquidity crunch has subsided. That can be difficult because central bankers are often combating perceived risks as much as they are real ones. For instance, Ben Bernanke and his fellow Fed policy makers were particularly active in late 2007 and throughout 2008, coordinating large-scale infusions of liquidity into the financial system and often using unusually creative mechanisms. But the credit market problems unleashed by the subprime lending debacle were large enough that interest rate cuts alone weren't enough. The central banks were signaling as strongly as they could that they wanted borrowers to access capital, that they were willing to let borrowers get access to capital at a lower cost, but for some reason that capital wasn't making its way into the economy. Perhaps banks needed to shore up the holes in their own balance sheeting, or borrowers, fearful of a looming recession, didn't want to take on new debt. Whatever the reason, money wasn't moving; there was negative liquidity. That kind of pattern, left unchecked, spells disaster for financial markets because it leads to volatile markets in which it's impossible for anyone to execute a purchase or sale of securities smoothly.

Central banks confronting this kind of crisis can jump-start the economy with a well-timed infusion of liquidity. But leaving that cash spigot turned on full force for a prolonged period of time is dangerous, because too much liquidity can create inflationary pressures that may prove equally hazardous. Central bankers now are all too aware of the risks of too much "easy money" (capital that is available at an interest rate that is lower than the growth in GDP). Indeed, it was the willingness of the Federal Reserve to accept that kind of interest rate policy beginning in early 2002 that set the stage for the biggest housing bubble in American history, complete with all the usual excesses:

investors using their homes as ATMs to mis-selling of poorly designed mortgage products.

Part of monitoring metrics, therefore, means keeping tabs on not only the direction of interest rates and economic growth, but on the relationship between them. When that relationship is taken to extremes, it spells trouble either for lenders or borrowers. For instance, a central bank that is keeping interest rates above the rate of GDP growth is sending a clear message that it doesn't want to risk the inflationary pressures that go hand in hand with low interest rates and so won't put money in investors' pockets with which the latter can speculate. That kind of gap between growth rates and lending rates means borrowers will have to be much more cautious in how they invest their own capital. The liquidity crunch makes its way throughout the financial system in this manner: As the Federal Reserve policy makers turn off the flow of cash, so investors respond by being picky about what they do with the smaller amounts they can afford to borrow, looking carefully through the array of possible investments for those they believe have the potential to grow at a faster clip than the overall economy. Those investments that don't meet their criteria will find investment capital hard to come by, and a liquidity crunch starts to take shape.

One way to detect liquidity problems is to monitor what is happening with the credit spreads that I discussed earlier. In the summer and fall of 2007, for instance, credit spreads widened suddenly and dramatically, as investors fled corporate bonds for the perceived safe haven of Treasury securities. That was a characteristic of an illiquid market, one in which corporate bonds and their issuers could offer higher and higher interest rates and yields without attracting buying interest. That's the reverse of the situation that prevailed between 2002 and 2007, when abundant liquidity, starting at the top with the central bank and its low interest rate policy, caused spreads to narrow between the yields on the most stable of assets (Treasury bonds) and securities issued by companies perceived as risky investments, either because they were laden with debt or had doubtful earnings growth prospects. The greater the amount of liquidity, the narrower the spread between these two groups; when cash is abundant, investors display a greater appetite for speculative securities. Therefore, when I want to understand how risk tolerant or risk averse investors are, credit spreads and the data they give me about credit risk can be helpful.

Why do I care how much appetite for risk investors have at any given moment? Because history has shown us that a growing appetite for risk—the kind that shows up in wider bond market spreads—tends to be linked to periods of healthy stock market returns. A host of specialized rating agencies assign ratings to every bond that is sold publicly to investors, with triple-A as the top rating (awarded to many government bonds and companies with perfect credit scores and pristine balance sheets). A double-A or single-A rating (or even an A minus) is still an investment-grade credit rating. But anything below a triple-B rating is viewed as much more speculative; many investors' guidelines ban them from buying these securities. But tracking the spread between the yields on these risky bonds and those of "risk-free" Treasury securities can tell me a lot about both liquidity and the appetite for risk on the part of the market as a whole. Between 1992 and 2007, for instance, 10-year corporate bonds with a speculative double-B rating yielded only about 2.4 percentage points more than 10-year Treasury notes; that's all that investors wanted in exchange for taking on the extra risk. Studying the historical performance of the Dow Jones Industrial Average, I found that whenever investors demanded more than 2.4 percentage points of extra yield before they would buy the BB-rated bonds, stock markets tended to struggle, returning only 2.6%.

The same Harris Private Bank study of the use of credit spreads as a market liquidity indicator suggested that credit was relatively easy and liquidity was flowing. In this case, liquidity served as an "environmental" indicator, telling us that liquidity was readily available enough that risk taking would be rewarded. In that kind of risk-taking environment, stocks are likely to fare well. So, I concluded after examining this study's results that a strong metrics-based argument seems to exist for staying invested in stocks when credit is easy and liquidity abundant, and for becoming cautious only when lenders begin to restrict credit. On the flip side, tighter credit conditions in the first half of 2008 suggested that investors were becoming risk averse and that making money in the stock market could be difficult (see Figure 9.2).

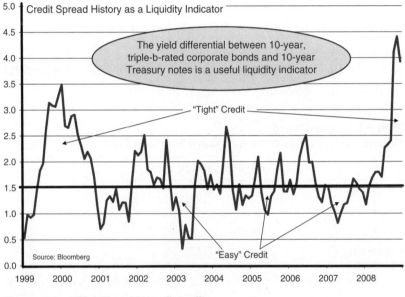

Figure 9.2   "Tight" and "easy" credit.

The study my team conducted at Harris Private Bank began by dividing the credit cycle into four phases. We defined the "expansion" phase as one where credit was tight and credit spreads were widening; the "peak" phase was characterized by tight credit and narrower credit spreads. In the "contraction" phase, credit was readily available as credit spreads narrowed. The "trough" phase saw easy credit and wider credit spreads. We reached back to June 1992, and put each month into one of those four categories. Then we calculated the performance of the Dow Jones Industrial Average for the 12-month period following each of those months.

The results confirmed our suspicions that credit and liquidity were reliable indicators of stock market out- or underperformance. The stock market fared worst after periods when credit had been tight: On average, the Dow returned 3.5% in the yearlong periods following an expansion reading and only 1.4% after peak phases. In contrast, when credit became readily available, the stock market tended to thrive. The Dow fared best after a contraction phase, with easy credit and narrower credit spreads, returning an average of 14.9% in subsequent yearlong periods. In the wake of a trough, the Dow returned an average of 13.3%. Trying to focus our study results on the essential question, we found that the Dow surged 14.2% in the wake of a period of easy credit conditions but only 2.6% after tight credit conditions (see Table 9.1).

TABLE 9.1   Dow Changes
Source: Harris Private Bank, Innovative Solutions Team

	Average 1-Year Change
Trough	13.3%
Expansion	3.5%
Peak	1.4%
Contraction	14.9%

The equation is straightforward. Narrow credit spreads are consistent with easy money. Easy money is another name for strong liquidity. For evidence, you don't have to look any further than the housing bubble. Lenders went overboard injecting liquidity into the real estate market from 2002 right through to the end of 2006, offering "teaser" rates, waiving down payments, and signing off on "liar" loans without verifying borrowers' incomes. Not surprisingly, the median price of a single-family home soared during the same period. Only when it became impossible to ignore the bubble did lenders pull in their horns, raise their lending standards, require higher credit scores, and even shut down lending to borrowers who didn't qualify. Credit spreads widened, liquidity evaporated, and the housing downturn worsened.

Wider spreads consistently signal that lenders are reluctant to extend credit—and they send a broader message that liquidity is constrained. This is true across a variety of markets, including stocks: Periods of wider credit spreads tended to correspond with monthly returns on the Dow Jones Industrial Average of only 0.8%. Whether that is due to a shortage of capital available to lend or to a general skittishness on the part of lenders, the result is that wider spreads drive up de facto borrowing costs and cause liquidity to evaporate.

So far, I have discussed liquidity metrics as a tool that can tell me when stock markets are poised to benefit from a flood of cash or credit markets likely to seize up as liquidity evaporates. However, these measurements can also prove useful when looking within the stock market. Understanding liquidity can help me evaluate the relative merits of different market sectors, such as whether larger blue-chip stocks appear likely to outperform their smaller counterparts, or vice versa. The kind of "little liquidity" I have described above—the willingness by investors to put their capital to work in riskier assets and asset classes—plays a role here, as well.

The stock market's abundant liquidity had a disproportionately positive impact on smaller-capitalization stocks. In absolute terms, this asset category can be seen as a riskier one in which to invest than larger businesses: Typically, a larger company has a broader range of business lines, a wider range of customers on whom to rely for sales and profits, greater access to capital, and a longer operating history. All these factors tend to reduce the perceived risk of investment in the eyes of money managers and others. But during the 5-year period between 2003 and 2007, bond markets compressed to an irrational degree and the small-cap stocks outperformed, beating blue-chips by 32%, or nearly 4% a year. Small-stock fund managers basked in the limelight and rejoiced in their returns, even as pundits predicted stubbornly, year after year, that *this* year would mark a return to life on the part of large-cap stocks.

By June 2007, small-cap stocks had celebrated a prolonged period of easy credit and outperformance, and the writing was on the wall. Investors seemed to remember the fundamental truth that in tougher times bankers are still going to be likely to trip over themselves to lend money to bulwarks of the economy like General Electric. But the same can't be said of lenders' attitudes to smaller stocks, such as a specialist retailer. Sure enough, lenders' fears that deteriorating subprime home loans would cause a slump in the corporate bond market spilled over into the stock market. Suddenly, lenders and investors alike decided they wanted to be compensated for the extra degree of risk associated with those asset classes and categories that tend to fall higher on the risk curve, from junk bonds to smaller-cap stocks. Market readjustments such as this are never easy and painless, but for small-cap stocks, the pain was worse: While the S&P 100 index of the largest U.S. stocks slid 2.5% between June and July 2007, the Russell 2000 Index (a broad measure of small-cap stock performance) slumped 6.9%.

Afraid of being caught on the wrong side of a flood of new liquidity, or of being left high and dry when liquidity evaporates overnight? You're not alone. So common are these fears—and the periods of ebullience and optimism that also characterize financial markets—you need to add investor psychology and market sentiment indicators to the list of factors to incorporate into your investment process, as I explain in the next chapter.

10

The Fourth Factor: Psychology— Greed Versus Fear

Sometimes what happens in the market just doesn't seem to make any sense at all.

We get up in the morning to find the sun is shining. Our vacation is scheduled to start on the weekend, and we feel pretty cheerful. Not only is our own life looking good, but there seems no reason for the stock market to burst our bubble. After all, fundamental valuations are reasonable, interest rates are relatively low, all the recent indicators of economic activity signal that growth is alive and well, and momentum metrics are sending positive signals.

And then it happens. As we watch, the market indexes dip a little, just a fraction of a percentage point. But with each hour that passes, the dip becomes larger. By midday, it's significant. The CNBC anchors are all abuzz, and major indexes have fallen a full percentage point. What's afoot? We call our brokers and investment advisors, only to find that they are just as baffled as we are. Should we worry? It's impossible not to—but *why?* As we fret, the relentless declines get worse. By the time the closing bell rings on the floor of the New York Stock Exchange, the major indexes have given up more than 2% of their value, all without any obvious cause! There's no giant corporate bankruptcy to point to, no piece of nasty and disappointing economic data to blame. Hmm, maybe it's time for us to jump on the bandwagon and begin to sell our own stocks?

What has just happened is that emotion has sent the stock market on an extreme rollercoaster ride and tested your nerve. You *shouldn't* worry about such short-term phenomena, but any time that a selloff drives the market below certain critical levels or whenever the rest of the investment world seems to be fighting to get out the same exit, it's hard to resist all that anxiety. None of our other metrics may be sending out warning signals, but everyone else is panicking as if the world is about to come to an end—and sometimes that is all that is needed to affect significantly the way a market moves.

That's the way irrationality creeps into the financial markets, and it happens more often than you might imagine (in both directions). What was rational about the trading day in mid-October 2008, when the Dow Jones Industrial Average swung more than 1,000 points in a single trading session—a record intra-day move at the time—only to close with a net change of less than 200 points? For all the scholarly research insisting that financial markets are rational places and that all known information is reflected in stock prices, when you're in the midst of an emotion-driven selloff or rally it's hard to keep your emotions isolated from your decision-making process. Investing remains an emotional process. I know, intellectually, that I need to buy when prices are low and sell when they are high, but it is unbelievably hard to do this. Time after time, I have found myself entranced by the Siren call of a bubble in the making, as I did in the mid-1980s during my brief flirtation with the idea of becoming a real estate investor, as I described in Chapter 8, "The Second Factor: The Economy— Headwind or Tailwind for Stocks?"

Being a contrarian, whether it means shunning bubble mania or embracing downturns, is never easy. When you have just watched the stock market wipe 5% off your total net worth in a single trading session, have lost 30% in the last few months investors found themselves in the dog days of autumn 2008, the idea that this might just be a great long-term buying opportunity sounds an awful lot like throwing good money after bad. All your instincts are screaming at you to take shelter from the stock market storm and protect yourself from further damage. Unexpected market declines like the one I described at the beginning of this chapter hurt not just your net worth, however, but also your confidence. And as I discussed in the introductory chapters of this book, most individual investors don't have a process governing their investment decisions and instead rely on what their gut is telling them about deciding when to buy or sell. Alas, the gut isn't a very reliable market indicator. It screams at you to pull back after you lose money and buy more as valuations soar. So, how can you make emotions a *manageable* part of your investment process? That is the focus of our fourth factor: market psychology, sentiment, and emotion. Collectively, the metrics I introduce you to here will help you filter others' emotions out of your investment decision-making process. And there is a bonus: Thinking about emotions in this analytical manner will help you remove your *own* emotions from the mix.

Although it took me another decade to begin thinking systematically about market psychology as a factor in its own right, I learned the hard way never to discount the impact of emotions on financial markets in October 1987. To those of us who experienced it firsthand, that was not only unforgettable but nearly unendurable. To this day, it remains the single most debilitating and helpless professional experience of my career, including the much more recent selloff of the autumn of 2008. (Back in 1987, an almost eerie mood of despair and confusion gripped all investors; this time around, curiously, many individual investors seemed to keep their heads. In 2008, the panicky selling came primarily from institutional investors, such as leveraged hedge funds, and although it was painful, it was spread over several weeks.) I'm sure that trading screens boasted more flashing red lights than the worst neighborhoods of Amsterdam and Bangkok combined. All any of us could do was to watch, in agony, as the stock market melted down in front of our eyes. With hindsight, I believe the loss of control hurt as much as the profit plunge. I felt as if I should somehow know how to survive a bear market. But I didn't have a clue. When the market finally closed on Black Monday, I left the office. On the street, I saw pedestrians crowded three deep looking at the electronic ticker displayed in brokerage office storefronts, trying to calculate the magnitude of the damage to their finances. Normally a hive of activity, the street outside my office that October day felt downright funereal. All of us felt we were witnesses to some kind of epochal event, along the lines of Pearl Harbor.

Astonishingly, those investors who responded to their instincts and fled for shelter in the coming days missed one of the biggest buying opportunities in stock market history. True, the S&P 500 Index didn't rebound immediately from its 22% loss in October, and in mid-December it was still lingering 5% below the closing price on Black Monday. But by the following February 1988, it was trading 10% higher above its November lows, and by the end of 1988 had soared 20% since Black Monday's close. A year later, at the end of 1989, the market had posted a 59% gain since the crash and was 15% ahead of its pre-crash levels. True, you would have had to be an automaton to be able to disregard the market's panic. But however emotional an investor may be, being able to rely on a process that addresses the risk and opportunities that emotion creates in the financial markets during times of turbulence is an investor with an edge. Only a process can help investors conclude whether a big market move is due to hysteria or some kind of shift in other factors. Only after you have drawn that conclusion can you decide how to assess the risks and rewards that appear and respond rationally.

Market psychology, like personal liquidity, is what I refer to as "landscape" factors. Although momentum or fundamentals can provide direct market signals that I can rely on when doing my primary analysis, these landscape factors tell me what is going on in the background that I can't afford to overlook. Just as politicians use opinion polls as a way to gauge the nation's mood and figure out what they can (or should) undertake with respect to their policies, investors need to pay attention to psychology. Indeed, if you look around you'll find lots of financial market equivalents of those surveys that you can incorporate into your decision-making process.

It wasn't until the aftermath of the dot.com bubble that I realized I needed to incorporate investor psychology into my own investment process in a formal way. I needed indicators that would signal when other such periods of irrational exuberance, to borrow the famous phrase used by former Federal Reserve Chairman Alan Greenspan, were taking shape. In January 2007, a metric that can serve as both a signal of liquidity and emotion appeared when the PIMCO Corporate Opportunity Fund, a closed-end fund that boasted a great deal of leverage, traded at a 15% premium to its net asset value. That told me that prospective investors were so eager to grab shares that they were willing to pay extra just to get into this fund. Was the risk really worth it? It was certainly a psychological red flag—investors were clearly casting caution to the winds. And sure enough, by October 2008, the fund was trading at a 15% *discount.*

If you're not convinced that you need to pay attention to emotion as a factor in its own right, just look at how the market reacted to Greenspan's use of that phrase. Sure, it unsettled investors for a day or two in late 1996. After that, investors tossed caution to the winds and sent valuations soaring for the next three years as they buzzed about a "new paradigm." Anyone who had been willing to examine the metrics that underpinned Greenspan's reasoning, however, would have known to heed market psychology closely over that subsequent period. Someone who responded to the underlying analysis over the long term rather than to the use of a particular phrase in the short term would have been prepared to detect the beginnings of the bear market early in 2000.

Just how much can emotional mood swings affect what happens to the market? Take a look at the annual returns posted by the stock market over the course of a year and compare that figure to the range in returns over the course of that year. During the 3-year period from 2000 to 2002, the 30 stocks in the Dow Jones Industrial Average lost ground steadily: 1.4% in 2000, 8% in 2001, and culminated in a 15.9%

drop in 2002. That was bad enough. But the pattern wasn't straight down, slowly and steadily. Instead, the market went on one of those nasty emotional rollercoaster rides. Over the course of 2000, the Dow Jones Industrial Average traded within an astonishingly wide 1,927-point range. In 2001, the intrayear trading range was an even wider 3,107 points, and it grew again to reach 3,349 points in 2002. So, to get to those losses—bad enough in their own right—stock market investors had to survive some nasty bouts of volatility. Anyone who tried to jump in or out at the wrong time could have ended up with a much worse investment performance.

It's never easy being a contrarian, especially when it requires you to step into the midst of a rout and start to buy. (In the lingo of stock market traders, that's called being prepared to "catch a falling knife.") Make no mistake, that's what I'm asking you to consider, because sometimes you need not just to step away from the crowd but run as far as you can in the opposite direction. Sure, a lot of the time, we'd all rather be wrong in company than right in isolation. Just take a look at some of the research that Jason Zweig cites in his book *Your Money and Your Brain*. In one study, neuroscientist Gregory Berns and his team asked test subjects to tell them whether two three-dimensional objects were the same as each other or different. When they were asked to make this decision as individuals, 84% of the test subjects got it correct. But when they were offered printouts from four different computers suggesting the wrong answer, their rate of accuracy dropped to only 68%. Placed in the company of four "peers," other individuals making the same erroneous recommendation, only 59% persisted in making the right decision. The inescapable conclusion is that the more you have to stand up for your views and confront others who insist on the opposite point of view, the harder it is to keep challenging the consensus. (Henry Fonda in *Twelve Angry Men* aside, the same phenomenon has been reported in jury rooms.) Zweig takes the analysis to an even higher level. Social isolation, he postulates, "activates some of the same areas of the brain that are triggered by physical pain. In short, you go along with the herd not because you consciously choose to do so, but because it hurts not to." Yes, that's right. I'm going to ask you to do exactly what Zweig's test subjects couldn't: to defy the herd. It may mean that you have to put up with some short-term pain (including ignoring all the persuasion brought to bear by your buddies at the gym or at cocktail parties). But that can boost the odds that you will outperform the market over the long haul. At the very least, by being able to monitor the market's emotional swings, you should be able to avoid being caught by either extremes of greed or fear.

Of course, as is the case in using each of these five factors, you will need to deploy the right metrics. The problem? Emotion is hard to quantify, and the kind of data you'll need to use isn't easily placed on a spreadsheet and subjected to quantitative analysis. For instance, one of those hard-to-measure metrics involves what topics or personalities national news magazines choose to feature on their cover pages. It has become somewhat commonplace to those in a given business or industry that when the latest development in their universe has appeared on the cover of *Time* or *Newsweek*, it signals that it is stale news or the investment opportunity has already been over-exploited. The truth is that publications such as these are victims of the "trickle-up" news phenomenon. They are trying to capture the biggest pieces of news nationwide. By the time a news item catches their attention, it has gone from being a regional or specialist phenomenon to something about which a wider audience is already aware. Take the July 29, 2002 cover of *BusinessWeek*, which sported the headline *The Angry Market* above a photograph of an alarmingly ferocious-looking bear. Dramatic, to be sure. But an investor who responded by shunning stocks would have forfeited the opportunity to profit from a 12% rally in the S&P 500 over the next 12 months.

Even the most prestigious publications are vulnerable to the same phenomenon. Consider the *Economist,* for instance. By the time it published a cover story on sovereign wealth funds in early 2008, these vast pools of capital from countries such as China, Saudi Arabia, and the Gulf principalities had been snapping up stakes in distressed U.S. investment banking firms for the better part of 2 months, and some were of the verge of pulling in their horns. In the midst of the telecommunications market slump in 2002, the *Economist* featured the news in a cover story only after most of the selloff had already happened, discussing its causes in its July 18, 2002 lead story, titled "The Great Telecom Crash." It turned out that the publication date of this story coincided eerily with the sector's cyclical low (to within days). How much stronger a contrarian indicator could you ask for? An investor who had purchased the telecom sector on the day the issue hit newsstands would have captured a return of nearly 9.5% by the end of the year. One of my favorite examples is the *Time* magazine cover of November 2, 1987. The title? "The Crash: After a wild week on Wall Street, the world is different." Well, yes and no. What the magazine intended to portray was the extent to which a heightened degree of risk aversion among investors would alter the long-term investment environment. All that had really changed, however, were valuations: The market had suddenly become considerably cheaper. So anyone who chose not to worry too much about the risk aversion that *Time* magazine discussed and who responded in a rational manner to this kind of market psychology by investing in stocks at their new lows would have made 65% over the next 5 years. This phenomenon—let's call it "the curse of the magazine cover"—isn't confined to the stock market. Back on June 15, 1987, *Time* sported a picture of the newly appointed Fed Chairman Alan Greenspan on its cover under the headline "The New Mr. Dollar." Early in his tenure, Mr. Greenspan commented that he thought the U.S. dollar, which had been slipping, was about to hit bottom and start to recover. Whoops! Within 12 months of the issue's publication, the greenback had plunged another 12.8% against a basket of foreign currencies (on a trade-weighted basis).

Headlines and the stories that run underneath them reflect investor sentiment. For unwary investors, market sentiment can be dangerous. For those able to develop metrics that capture investor psychology, however, studying emotional indicators like this can help navigate the market's most bullish or bearish time frame. That's because those indicators are useful in indicating the level of risk associated with a particular asset class or market at any given point in time. One cautionary note: Investor psychology metrics alone aren't an adequate basis for undertaking an asset-allocation shift or investment decision any more than metrics linked to the other "landscape" factor, liquidity. Instead, you should rely on other factors (momentum, the economy, or fundamentals) for those buy or sell signals, and then turn to market psychology in search of confirmation. If the economic environment is bearish and fundamentals seem the same, but psychology metrics are bullish, that's not enough to turn bullish. It does mean that you need to take a hard look at those other metrics and reevaluate them in the light of the bullish sentiment reading.

Many investor psychology measurement tools are readily available to individual investors. In each week's issue of *Barron's*, there is a sentiment indicator devised and overseen by the American Association of Individual Investors. (This Chicago-based nonprofit was established in 1978 to educate and help individual investors managing their own portfolios.) Every week, the group polls its 100,000 members, asking them what they expect from the stock market over the next 6 months. Member responses are categorized as bullish, bearish, or neutral and expressed as a percentage of all responses. (A relatively bearish sentiment indicator would be a response of 31%, for instance, while a 46% reading would signal relative bullishness.) Shortly after Bloomberg first made the survey results available on their terminals in 1987, I began trying to develop a trading strategy based on it. My team and I established a series of trading ranges, from "relative bullishness" to "relative bearishness," using the levels of optimism and pessimism in the index as contrarian indicators. When bullish sentiment dipped below 31%, our strategy would send us a buy signal. We'd continue to remain upbeat about the stock market as long as the level of bullish sentiment remained below 46%. As soon as it broke above that point, however, we were officially in the realm of excessive bullishness, suggesting that it was time to sell. I confess that this approach to investing didn't make me fabulously wealthy. I would have been better off just buying and owning a broad market index over the long haul. Testing this market psychology–based trading strategy over the 20-year period between 1987 and 2007, I found that an initial investment of $1,000 put to work during periods of bearishness and withdrawn when the bulls ran amok produced $5,025, or an annualized return of 8.2%. Just buying and holding the 30 stocks in the Dow Jones Industrial Average would have given me an 8.4% annualized return, or about $5,186 for every $1,000 invested, over the same time period (see Figure 10.1). (Although, of course, it's pretty hard for most investors to buy and hold a stock portfolio without succumbing to the temptation to tweak those positions for two decades!)

Figure 10.1   Growth of $1,000 invested in the Dow Jones Industrial Average.

But beyond the fact that this strategy produced more than adequate investment returns, our contrarian approach resulted in a less-volatile and thus less-risky portfolio. Over the 20-year study period, the Dow posted an annualized standard deviation of 15.7%—the "normal" level of stock market volatility. Moving in and out of the market in response to bullish or bearish signals, however, produced nearly the same returns, with an annual standard deviation of only 11.8% (a better risk-adjusted performance). So someone defying the crowd and adopting a contrarian investment strategy would have earned nearly as much over a long period of time (and would have been able to sleep better at night).

There are a number of different ways to gauge how skittish, or how exuberant, investors feel about a financial market, especially when it comes to the stock market. Take the Chicago Board Option Exchange's VIX Index, for instance. The index, often referred to during the market turmoil of the fall of 2008 during CNBC talkfests, is simply a way to measure the volatility of stocks in the S&P 500. Specifically, it measures the perception of investors in options on the index with respect to the index's volatility over the coming 30 days. (An investor will buy or sell different kinds of options at different prices if he is expecting a very volatile market than he will buy if he predicts a quiet few weeks.) The VIX is calculated by backing out the volatility assumptions in the prices of all actively traded index options. The CBOE has been tracking volatility data since 1990, because that information is vital to any investor trying to calculate the value of an option contract. The rest of us don't need to trade options to find this data useful. The lower market volatility is, as measured by the VIX, the more likely investors are to be complacent. The reverse is also true: When volatility spikes higher, investors tend to be more nervous and wary of committing their capital to what they may view as a riskier asset class.

Over the lifetime of the VIX (as of the date I write this in early 2009), S&P 500 volatility has fallen as low as 10% in early 2007, meaning that at the time, a majority of investors believed the annual return—or the loss—of the S&P 500 wouldn't exceed 10% in either direction. But in August 1998, at the height of the emerging markets debacle and in the wake of the collapse of Long Term Capital Management, fear drove the index to a record high of 44%, suggesting investors believed that two-thirds of the time, the S&P 500's annual return would remain within plus or minus 44% (an astonishingly wide range). If you look at those two dates, however, the figures aren't very surprising. In early 2007, investors were still celebrating the end of a year that had rewarded them with a 15% jump in the S&P 500 and returns that had totaled some 75% over the past 4 calendar years. Not surprisingly, they were pretty content. Of course, as we all came to realize over the next 2 years, there was a lot to worry about just waiting in the wings. The subprime lending debacle was about to explode in the financial markets, economic growth was about to slow, and within a year everyone was worried about the prospect of a recession. A great example of a contrarian indicator at work! The signal worked the same way in 1998; investors were naturally uncertain and even downright fearful that summer after a yearlong slide in the Asian emerging markets followed by that year's shocking decision by the Russian government to default on its debt payments. Between July 15 and August 30, the S&P 500 plunged 20%, and investor angst ran so high that the stage was set perfectly for a dramatic rebound. The market complied: The S&P surged more than 20% between Labor Day and New Year's Day of 1999.

Like all data, the VIX is nothing more than a collection of numbers until you find a way to analyze and use the data it gives you. Spotting the contrarian link between volatility and market performance, I decided to try using the VIX as a kind of complacency indicator: The lower the level of volatility, the greater the level of complacency and vice versa. In a study I conducted of the VIX's behavior between January 1990 and December 2008, I categorized each month-end volatility reading as "high" and the market as nervous if the VIX ran above 25%, "medium" when it hovered between 15% and 25%, and "low" (or complacent) when the index fell below 15%. For every period in which the VIX registered as high, medium, or low levels, my research team and I studied the market's performance over the following 6 months. The result: The greater the volatility, the higher the returns over the coming months. Indeed, high volatility periods were followed by average monthly returns for S&P 500 stocks of 6.3%. Because volatility tends to peak during the times when financial markets hit rock bottom and the last bulls throw in the towel, that isn't too surprising. Once the die-hard bulls have capitulated, long-term investors often find the best buying opportunities, just as those of us who were investing two decades ago saw in the aftermath of the 1987 stock market crash.

In contrast, low-volatility periods during which investors bragged about their recent returns and felt unworried about the future of their investments (as indicated by the fact that they didn't tweak their portfolios much in response to market event events) were followed by an average return of 5.4% over the succeeding 6-month period. Curiously, periods of medium volatility were characterized by the lowest returns in the subsequent 6 months (only 1.7%—see Figure 10.2). Perhaps these represent markets in transition. Obviously, this data isn't robust enough for you to base your entire investment strategy on it (as indeed you shouldn't use investor psychology metrics as the basis for your investment process), but it's a good indicator of what kind of information you can glean from psychology data points.

By now, you probably have a pretty good idea of the kind of metric you are looking for in order to incorporate this factor into your decision-making process. You want data that tells you when people are really pessimistic, or at least tells you the degree of pessimism that seems to be in the market. If your analysis of the economy, momentum, and fundamentals tells you that a market is a buy, a great signal confirming that it's time to hit the buy button and shift some assets into the stock market would be some data showing that other folks out there are feeling grumpy. Almost anything that measures relative

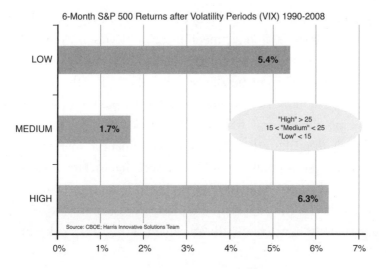

Figure 10.2   Returns after periods of volatility.

levels of pessimism and optimism is fair game. For instance, I tracked the UBS Index of investor optimism on a monthly basis from February 1999 through to the end of December 2007 (when it ceased publication), an index based on survey data that UBS compiled with the help of Gallup based on polls of investors with total savings and investment accounts of $10,000 or more randomly selected across the United States. Yet again, the data showed that higher levels of bearishness were followed by periods of higher returns. The UBS Index may no longer be available to us, but other indicators are. For instance, the New York Stock Exchange monitors the extent to which investors are so bearish about individual stocks that they actually place trades betting that their prices will fall (a process referred to as short selling). Briefly, when investors sell a stock short, they are selling a stock they have "borrowed" from an investment dealer or brokerage firm, hoping or expecting that when they replace that stock it will be trading at a lower price. Let's say that an investor was able to sell that borrowed stock for $90 a share and buys it back 3 months later for $60. The $30 price difference is profit. The NYSE tracks how much short selling is going on in the stocks it lists and publicly discloses each month the stocks with the largest "short interest ratio."

(That ratio is calculated using the average daily trading volume in the individual stock against the number of shares of that stock sold short.) The result is the "days to cover" ratio, telling us how many days of trading it would take for those bearish positions to disappear if they were unwound.

The stock exchange goes one step further, publishing similar data for all the stocks it lists in aggregate. I have found that a big change in the short interest ratio can correspond to a shift in investor sentiment and foreshadow a change in the market's direction. As with all other psychology metrics, it's all about being contrarian: The more short selling going on, the more nervous investors are likely to be. A high level of short interest in the market may signal that all the bears have already succumbed. (That's a risky bet, requiring a higher-than-usual level of conviction, because if investors get it wrong their downside is potentially unlimited. Think for a moment about what would have happened to our hypothetical speculator of a few moments ago, who sold borrowed stock at $90 a share, only to watch its price soar to $120, $150, or $180! As long as he doesn't close out that short position by buying back the stock at the new, higher price, his losses on the trade are potentially infinite.) You may recall the way in which Google shares exploded on to the market after their initial public offering. A handful of New York hedge funds, skeptical about the company's performance (perhaps they remembered what happened to the last batch of high-flying technology stocks), sold Google shares short. It was a painful experience for them. Google's stock doubled, tripled, and ultimately quadrupled.

A high short interest ratio tells market veterans more than just the fact that the bears are running amok. Rather, it's an early warning signal that the bulls may be about to return to the fray. In fact, the two species actually become one and the same for a brief moment in time. Once everyone who is bearish on the market has established a short position—driving short interest ratios high—how much new selling is likely to materialize? At that point, paradoxically, the bears represent a source of new buying because, at some point, they will decide to close out their positions and collect their profits. Because closing out those positions means buying the stock, that increased demand can translate into an uptick in the stock's price as demand exceeds supply. And when the first shorts cover their positions, the upward jump in prices triggers a response among their peers, fearful of being the last to get out of their positions. So they're likely to react like lemmings and start buying back stock, too, fearful of being caught in what's known as a short squeeze (defined as the painful position short sellers find themselves in when their bet goes wrong and the stock price climbs rather than falls). No one wants to be squeezed by a bull.

None of the indicators I'm describing here should be used in isolation, including the NYSE short interest ratio. Ideally, you should monitor what is happening with all these metrics and look for a point when they all seem to be generally in agreement about the level of pessimism or optimism in the stock or bond markets. Some of the data sets that I've seen people use in the pursuit of an insight into the collective psychology of investors can be tricky to use with any conviction. For instance, buying or selling of stock by insiders (defined by the Securities and Exchange Commission as people likely to have access to privileged information about a company's business and prospects, such as senior managers and board members) is a favorite tool many investors use to calculate bullish sentiment. The theory is great: Company insiders (who have the most knowledge about the business) will buy when they believe their company's shares are undervalued and less well-informed investors are underestimating its potential growth in earnings and revenues. But insiders aren't like other investors. They typically have a lot of their net worth tied up in company stock and get more each year as part of their compensation. So insiders might be selling purely to diversify their own portfolios, pay for their children's private-school tuition, or to buy a ski chalet in Vermont. Automatically assuming that selling is bearish is wrong.

Most sentiment or psychology metrics apply to the stock market, but other, more specialized sentiment data is available for other markets. Consensus, a sentiment research firm, conducts weekly surveys of money managers on a variety of markets, including crude oil, gold, and silver. Jeffery Weniger, one of my research assistants at Harris Private Bank, studied crude oil sentiment data between April 1985 and July 2004, and rated readings above 75 as bullish, those below 25 as bearish, and those in between as neutral. A familiar pattern emerged. In the wake of a bullish period, crude oil's price tended to drop 5.6% in the following 6 months. When they were bearish, the average return in the next 6 months was 12%. (A neutral reading was followed by an average 3.2% return.)

The problem you'll face in dealing with psychology metrics won't be trying to find enough data. Thankfully, even analyzing it is relatively straightforward, especially when compared to some of the more complex metrics used in connection with other factors. Indeed, any problems you face are likely to be because of the people who generate those data sets, since people are, well, people. Let's face it, we are notoriously bad at figuring out what we feel and why we feel that way. (How else to explain the popularity of psychiatrists in North America?) In particular, we collectively tend to be very bad judges of how we are going to feel in the future. Myriad studies tell me that I will overestimate how much pain I'll suffer at the dentist's as well as the delight I'll experience during my much-anticipated Mexican vacation. (Perhaps I mentally block out the fact that while the dentist offers pain relief, sunburn and bouts of Montezuma's revenge can wreak havoc on the best-planned holiday.) As a kid, I was one of the last people in Chicago to see the original *Star Wars* movie after it opened in the 1970s. By the time I did, I was ready for something extraordinary, thanks to the buzz. Leaving the cinema, I felt let down. Sure, the special effects were impressive, but I never understood what was going on. I'm not alone; studies show that anyone who sees a movie or reads a book before reading a bunch of positive reviews or hearing too many friends' opinions tends to enjoy it more and rate it more highly. In my experience, the flip side is true as well. Poor expectations tend to set the bar very low. Anyone who decides to flout conventional thinking and attend a film or read a book that received poor reviews is more likely to be pleasantly surprised. Think about this next time the market anticipates a poor employment report from the Labor Department. The lower the expectation, the better the odds are for a positive surprise.

That's why, tempting as it might be to ignore my advice, I urge you not to succumb to the temptation to use market sentiment indicators such as the ones I've shared with you as the primary factor in your decision-making process, much less the only one. Yes, these metrics offer valuable clues into the way investors are thinking, as measured by their behavior in buying, selling, and short selling stocks. But the biggest mistake you can make is to *automatically* be a contrarian. Although it's rare to find a market full of bears that is also overvalued, it's not impossible, particularly in the early stages of a market correction. There's little that is as painful as finding yourself stuck in a value trap—a supposedly cheap stock (as measured by market psychology or some other metric) that just keeps getting cheaper and cheaper and....

And that is the very reason that fundamentals play such a critical role in shaping any robust investment process.

11

The Fifth Factor: Fundamentals and Valuation

The investment universe is chockablock with opportunities. Wherever you turn, something new grabs your attention. Interested in a portfolio of battered subprime securities? A stake in the newest emerging economies in countries such as Vietnam and Kazakhstan? If you feel like putting your spare cash to work in a wind farm in Brazil or your brother-in-law's new gourmet sandwich shop, you can take that risk, or you can opt for the lower-risk alternative of purchasing short-term Treasury bills, even if they provide as little yield as they do risk. Each of these options offers a unique set of risk and return characteristics you need to analyze before you write a check or complete the electronic funds transfer. Although the first four factors that I have discussed can help you navigate your way through a noisy market environment and gauge the best time to make an asset-allocation shift, you need to be able to make your own decision about which particular investment offers the best combination of risk and return—the best fundamentals. And that is where my fifth and final factor (valuation) comes into play.

"Relative valuation" is the single most important criterion in determining how you will separate the most attractive markets from the ones that are only mildly interesting and those that are downright unattractive. Regardless of the type of investment you're mulling—that sandwich shop, say, or blue-chip U.S. stocks—valuation tools will help you make an objective decision. That becomes particularly crucial the more volatile and fast moving markets become, when emotions distort asset prices. The more you focus on metrics that help you identify asset classes that are over- or undervalued, the more opportunities you have to outperform. Take the autumn of 2008, when Wall Street held a yard sale. Indeed, prices were so low in one of the worst market blowouts in decades that valuation issues became almost academic. Hedge funds and other investors who had bought their holdings with borrowed money that they now were being told to repay pronto hit the "sell" button over and over again. It wasn't just stocks that suffered; the prices of high-quality bonds were battered so severely that their yields (which move in the opposite direction to prices; the cheaper a bond gets, the more attractive its coupon becomes when calculated as a percentage of the current price) became downright enticing. Since 1996, lenders have historically asked for and received about 1.6 percentage points of extra yield in the shape of higher interest rates in exchange for purchasing a triple-B rated corporate bond rather than a Treasury bond. After the rout of autumn 2008, however, the same triple-B corporate bonds offered an astonishing 4.6 percentage points of extra yield! By historic standards, the corporate securities were the valuation equivalent of finding a bona-fide designer handbag for sale for $50 at your local Wal-Mart.

In the early stages of the credit crunch that wreaked havoc on financial markets in 2008 and into 2009, several strategists believed that the emerging markets would offer some form of shelter from the mayhem. Emerging market economies, these optimists argued, would hold out because they were less connected to the global economy, so when the United States sneezed, they wouldn't catch cold. I wasn't so sure, as I told investors early in 2008. The problem? Even if they managed to hold out against the tide, emerging markets were, as an asset class, relatively expensive when measured against the S&P 500. The MSCI Emerging Markets Index boasted a price/earnings ratio of 15 early in 2008, while the S&P traded at 18.2 times earnings.

Yet as recently as March 2002, the price/earnings ratio of the emerging markets was only a third of that of the S&P 500; its relative value had exploded over the previous 6 years, reflecting analysts' conviction that growth prospects for corporate earnings in the emerging markets were higher than those in the developed markets. The arguments appeared compelling, but I resisted, for which I would be very thankful later. I was going to assume that the emerging markets stock universe was overpriced until some set of indicators proved otherwise; however, it was also wise to maintain some emerging market exposure for long-term growth and diversification.

Think about the ways in which valuation fundamentals affect a decision most of us face a few times in our lives: whether to buy a new house. Imagine that it's the summer of 2008, you have just retired, and you are considering a move to Miami so that you can play golf throughout the year. You've even found the right house, and it's priced at a discount! Your friends, however, think you're nuts. "Haven't you noticed the real estate market is crashing?" they demand. And they are right. Between December 2006 and August 2008, the value of the average home in the Miami area plunged about 30% in the midst of one of the worst localized housing crashes in American history. But that, along with your desire to live a 10-minute drive from scores of enticing golf courses, is just "noise." The bigger and more important question you have to address is whether the fundamentals make sense. Is the property fairly valued? If it is very cheap compared to recent sales, you need to figure out why that is, and then whether the current price really represents good value. To answer the question of value, you need metrics that will help you understand the real estate market and the relative value of the home you are proposing to buy.

Your primary consideration should be the fundamentals: Is the home appropriately priced for its condition, its age, its location, as compared to the prices at which other similar houses have changed hands? If the answer is yes, you can think about what the other four factors tell you about both the investment itself and the timing. For instance, the economy may play a role in your decision: If the dollar's value is low, this might lure foreign buyers in search of winter sun into the Florida real estate market. Understanding the market's psychology will also help you: After such a plunge in real estate values, there are few buyers, meaning that prices may be discounted. The liquidity factor may also be on your side. If you have a solid credit rating and can make a sizeable down payment, you might be able to finance the purchase even as 60% of banks are scaling back their lending. Momentum may be another green light. The supply of houses in Florida has exploded over the past decade or so as property developers adopted a "build it and they will come" approach; now many sit empty. These four factors are crucial. But at the end of the day, if fundamental indicators tell you value isn't there in the first place, the rest is academic.

Thinking about investment fundamentals always makes me think about exactly how I earn returns for investors. These returns come either in the form of income (interest payments on bond investments or stock dividends, for instance) or capital appreciation (an increase in the market value of the securities I buy). The goal of valuation metrics is to calculate what kind of income I'm likely to earn and the probability of appreciation or depreciation, measured against the prevailing market price. What price am I being asked to pay for a stream of income, or yield? What is the cost today of what I expect will be a 20% gain in the S&P 500 over the next 2 years? Is the price fair, when compared to other potential investments? This way, I put all available opportunities on a level playing field and am able to make sense of asset classes that may have very different risk and return characteristics, such as bonds and commodities. In all cases, I'm trying to use valuation metrics to decide whether an investment that looks like a bargain *is* a bargain.

In the world of bonds, where I began my investment career, valuation issues were fairly straightforward. What matters to bond investors is the price they pay for each issue, together with the issuer's credit quality. The first step is to calculate whether the current market price for the bond you're looking at is at a discount to the price at which it was issued. That's pretty easy to do, because most bonds are issued at what's called "par" value, or the principal amount that investors will receive when the bond matures in 3, 5, 10, or more years. (Most often, that is $1,000.) Once issued, the bond's price fluctuates in response to a complex set of interconnected factors ranging from the issuer's credit quality and cash-flow outlook to interest rate levels. But the real question for an investor—as opposed to a trader—involves a simple mathematical calculation. Is the company making enough money to make its interest and principal payments to investors on time and in full? The bet is a binomial one: Either the bond paid off or it didn't. If the cash was there, and you could buy the bond at a discount, you won over its lifetime. If not, you would lose.

Leaving this black-and-white universe for the Technicolor world of stock market analysis, I had to rethink my approach to investment fundamentals in light of the seemingly endless range of scenarios and outcomes that stocks offered. Will a company hit or miss its quarterly earnings forecast? What if its largest rival achieves a technological breakthrough? Is the company an acquisition target, and can the buyer finance the transaction? Will its chief financial officer cook the books and run off to Tahiti? All of these considerations (and more) play a role in shaping a company's stock price and thus its market value. Next comes the complex question of whether that market value is appropriate, one made trickier by the fact that stocks—unlike the vast majority of fixed-income investments—don't ever mature, and few offer much in the way of yield. (Not all publicly traded companies opt to pay dividends on their common stock, and those dividends that do exist can fluctuate greatly.)

But like all markets, the stock market offers tremendous opportunities to perceptive and disciplined investors. Indeed, each surge of emotion, and each lurch in market indexes when momentum temporarily displaces common sense, creates a fresh opportunity for this small group of investors. Sometimes these opportunities are dramatic. By the late 1990s, the giant surge in technology stocks created an outsize valuation gap between technology and telecommunications stocks and almost every other sector. Long-term investors known for their keen eye for market values were left in the dust. By early 2000, Berkshire Hathaway, the holding company that serves as the vehicle through which famed value investor Warren Buffett invests in businesses he believes are undervalued, was trailing the broader stock market by an astounding 50% on an annual basis. In March of that year, hedge fund investor Julian Robertson, another value investing devotee, shuttered his Tiger Fund. Both men publicly voiced their skepticism about the astronomically high valuations investors were ascribing to Internet-related stocks. Sure enough, those investors who trusted their observations about valuation and had the courage to act on them by slashing their technology stock holdings and shifting the proceeds into "value" stocks ended up outperforming their peers for several years to come. Meanwhile, those who argued that the advent of the Internet meant that the fundamental valuation rules had been repealed were left with large losses.

It's not easy to be a contrarian. In the case of technology stocks, the market defied fundamental valuation indicators for years before the break occurred. Even in more normal times, markets can become excessively bullish or bearish for months at a time. Investors aren't required to buy when the market is cheap or sell when it becomes pricey. Still, to manage their risk and pursue returns, they need to know where in that valuation cycle they stand.

Valuation metrics include some of the stock market's most familiar indicators, all of which will help investors separate good investment ideas from those that are bad or merely indifferent. I divide them into three types. The most widely used are those linking the price of a security, index, or other investment to an item on a company's income statement, such as revenue or profits. By far the best known of these is the ubiquitous price/earnings (or P/E) ratio. (Others include price-to-cash flow and price-to-sales ratios, and the earnings yield.) Next comes a group of valuation metrics tying the security's market price to something on the balance sheet, such as the price-to-book value ratio. The third category includes yield-oriented measurements, such as dividend yield or yield to maturity.

When I began overseeing stock portfolios, I realized that the valuation methodology I used would depend on the kind of decision I was going to make, and that not all indicators would work. I knew I shouldn't obsess over whether or not pharmaceutical giant Pfizer's valuation was appropriate, for all the reasons that I outlined early in this book. Besides, that was for our analysts to decide. Why worry only about the fundamentals of Pfizer's new drugs? For every pharma company with a poor new drug pipeline, there is another that has a blockbuster product just awaiting approval. What I needed in place of Pfizer-specific metrics or even some kind of insight into the complexities of the FDA's new drug approval process was a broader indicator telling me whether the valuation of the pharmaceutical industry looked attractive when measured against all the other possible industries in which I could invest. Generally speaking, I needed the most general valuation metrics I could find; the ones that would help me identify times when entire asset classes were overvalued or undervalued. Moreover, some metrics have only limited utility. For instance, cash-flow analysis can prove very useful in looking at the banking and financial services arena, but it simply isn't relevant when you take a step back from sectors and try to look at comparing valuations among asset classes. When I took over the BankBoston asset-allocation fund and had to decide which asset class to invest in at any given time to generate the best return for my clients, I realized that the valuation tools I needed most were those best able to capture broader valuation gaps between asset classes.

The most crucial "fundamental" metric proved to be the earnings yield model, thanks to its ability to help me calculate the relative merits of stocks and bonds at any given point in time. Also known as the Fed model (a nod to its genesis in the Federal Reserve Board of Alan Greenspan's era), it looks like an upside-down price/earnings ratio.

The P/E ratio divides the price of a stock, index, or other security by the expected or actual earnings for that asset and ends up with a number that can be compared to the security's peers, industry, or the market as a whole. In contrast, the Fed model begins by taking analysts' forecasts for the operating earnings of the companies in the S&P 500 for the coming 12 months. You then divide that sum by the current price of the S&P Index itself. (The same model can, of course, be applied to any other stock index.) The result? An earnings yield for the index. If you take that earnings yield and put it on a chart against the current interest rate that an investor could capture by investing in the 10-year Treasury bill, you'll see an easy-to-understand comparison of the relative allure of stocks and bonds.

This metric offers a simple way to combine earnings, prices, and interest rates to reach this conclusion. When the earnings yield is significantly above the Treasury yield, the Fed model tells me that investors are very pessimistic about stocks and are demanding to be paid an outsize amount of yield in return for the risk of investing in them. The stock market's earnings yield can fall below Treasury yields in a bull market, telling you that investors aren't worried about stock market risk and don't feel any need for the kind of safe haven that triple-A government bonds offer. Edward Yardeni, an economist and strategist at Deutsche Bank in New York during the late 1990s, paid a lot of attention to the Fed model during this period. It proved popular when it not only served as a reliable indicator of past bull and bear market cycles but also provided clear signals that the bull market of the late 1990s was heading for disaster—the ultimate asset-allocation call, for those who were alert enough to catch it. By the first quarter of 2000, the model suggested that the stock market was 70% overvalued. Sure enough, within weeks, the S&P 500 had begun the nosedive that would wipe 40% off the value of the large-cap stock universe over the next 3 years. Midway through this painful period, in the summer of 2001, I joined Harris Private Bank. By then, I was running the Fed model calculations every month. I was sure that just as it had given an early warning of the market meltdown to come, so it would warn me when stocks finally ended up trading too cheaply relative to bonds. It took a while for this to happen, as the terrorist attacks of September 11, 2001 further damaged an already weak economy and the gloom deepened and spread. By the time major stock indexes hit bottom in the third quarter of 2002, one of the worst periods for stock investors in half a century (at that time), the bears were running the show. Even without a dramatic crash of the kind seen in 1987 and later, in the fall of 2008, by the time investors closed their books on September 30, the S&P had fallen 17.3% in only 3 months. For most of the people working on trading desks or running mutual funds, it would be the single most painful period they had experienced first-hand thus far and wouldn't be matched for another 6 years.

So it wasn't exactly the perfect time to try making a bullish case for stocks. No one wanted to stick their neck out in an environment like that; everyone who had tried to bet on a turnaround in stocks had lost a lot of money and credibility. Nonetheless, the Fed model had begun to send out signals that I couldn't ignore. A string of interest rate cuts designed to battle the recession had driven Treasury market yields lower, and stocks were now somewhere between 20% and 30% undervalued. An investment opportunity had been created. Bracing myself, I recommended to our investment policy committee that we should sell bonds and buy stocks until stock market exposure was above the target. For weeks after I made the call, I traveled from one Harris Private Bank office to the next, reinforcing my recommendation to individual portfolio managers. I knew it was a risky decision, but the credibility of my work was on the line—not only with our clients, but with our portfolio managers as well.

Of course, the Fed model isn't infallible. Critics have argued that it's a good short-term indicator but that it doesn't provide long-term signals and that Treasurys aren't the best assets to compare to stocks. I agree on both counts, although that flaw doesn't mean the metric is useless. As long as you remember that it works best when you're trying to understand valuation fundamentals for the coming 12 to 18 months, you can still treat it as a very useful gauge of the relative valuations of the two key asset classes, stocks and bonds. If you believe that Treasury bonds are too low risk to be compared to stocks, you'll find that it's easy to substitute the yield on an index made up of triple-B rated corporate bonds for the rate on the 10-year Treasury. Even with these changes and caveats, the Fed model still emerges as the single best way to tackle the first valuation decision any investor will face: whether stocks or bonds offer the greatest upside potential.

The Fed model isn't the only valuation metric that can help with this critical choice between stocks or bonds. An alternative is the dividend discount model, which calculates all the future dividend flows that the components of a given stock index can be estimated to produce in perpetuity. It's like the P/E ratio, with the difference that investors actually receive dividends; so it measures the cash return for the index. How much would you want to pay to own that flow of income? Most investors would prefer to purchase it at a discount. So, if you compare the discounted yield to the current market price for those securities, that will give you useful information about the best strategy to pursue. It's a fairly straightforward calculation: I know or can calculate future dividend payments; I know the current market value and can therefore calculate the implied rate of growth. The glitch, of course, is that dividends aren't fixed and that not all stocks pay dividends these days. So replacing dividend growth with some measure of long-term earnings growth is a sensible alternative. Doing so means you can capture the anticipated long-term growth in the stock index—that growth is a key objective for any stock investor—and compare that to current market pricing.

These two models are just the starting point, a way to help me understand whether stocks or bonds look more attractive based on valuation fundamentals. But that simply opens the door to a series of fresh questions that must now be addressed, using similar or completely different valuation metrics. It's a bit like having to make a choice between planning a summer vacation in the Loire Valley in France or California's Napa Valley. Concluding the exchange rate isn't in your favor and that hotel bills and other expenses would put too big a dent in the family budget, you decide on California. Now you face an array of new decisions. Will you fly to San Francisco, or put the family in the car and drive? Which airline will you take, and does it make sense to use your frequent-flyer miles? Once there, will you head for a campsite or a boutique bed and breakfast? Working your way through your investment process with valuation metrics isn't that different. When you've made the decision that stocks look relatively more attractive than bonds and other asset classes, you have decided on your direction and destination. Implementing that, and building a portfolio that reflects that decision, means you have to decide which *part* of the stock market offers the best opportunities. Which valuation metrics will help you figure out whether the U.S. stock market is the best option, or whether you want to steer a greater percentage of your nest egg into overseas stock markets?

Too often, investors miss a step in their thought processes at this point in the analysis. Once they've concluded that stocks are the better bet, they move straight past the next logical question (Which stock markets offer the best potential returns?) and instead decide which U.S. market sectors they should emphasize in their portfolios. That's surprising, given the ever-increasing array of global investment opportunities that become more and more accessible to individual investors each year. Once, "global" investing meant buying American Depository Receipts (U.S.-listed securities) of a few giant European multinational concerns. These days, not only do domestic European markets offer much more diversity, but emerging markets ranging from China to Poland and South Africa provide exposure to new kinds of businesses aimed at exploiting entirely new opportunities. A fresh category, the so-called frontier markets, such as Vietnam and Nigeria, are beginning to attract the attention of institutional investors and ultimately will be accessible to the most risk tolerant of individual investors. You can still use U.S. stocks as the benchmark and see how European, Russian, or Mexican stock markets compare in terms of valuation; the key is to keep an open mind when you're looking for the best opportunity on the basis of fundamentals.

It's true that more Americans own more non-U.S. stocks in their portfolios than at any time in history, reflecting the diminishing size of the U.S. stock market as a percentage of the global equity universe. (Today, U.S. stocks make up about slightly less than half of the $30 trillion in global equities, compared to about 60% two decades ago.) Unfortunately, too often those investments are made without thinking about relative valuation: Investors are using a bottom-up approach and deciding to pull money out of another investment and put it to work in, say, China's hottest retail stock after reading a story about the growth of the Chinese consumer market. Instead, they should be thinking carefully and strategically about the Chinese stock market and the opportunities it offers in relation to the investment being sold to provide the cash to buy that hot stock. Where does the best valuation opportunity present itself? And where do valuations appear overstretched?

But with literally dozens of such disparate stock markets to sort through, how can an investor find a way to make a relative valuation decision? Forget about apples-to-apples comparisons; this is more like trying to compare cabbages to kiwis. Here's where the venerable price/earnings ratio, or P/E ratio, comes into its own. I'm not suggesting that you allocate your entire equity portfolio to the ten markets with the lowest price/earnings ratios—that would be like using a howitzer to deal with an annoying mosquito. Indeed, if you rely only on the P/E ratio, you risk shunning higher-growth markets (which typically have higher P/E ratios) in favor of those that are more volatile and risky (which tend to have lower P/E ratios)—a far from sensible strategy.

At the same time, finding some way to compare the valuation of one asset class or category to another is vital because each dollar you invest in any one group of stocks or bonds is a dollar no longer available to invest elsewhere. So when you're making the decision about what to do with that dollar, relative valuation becomes vital. Tune into Bloomberg radio or CNBC, and you'll hear television pundits debating a particular stock's valuation metrics and how such and such a price/earnings ratio or book value or dividend yield makes it cheap and thus attractive as an investment. But by itself, the assertion that Pfizer, for instance, is "cheap" tells you nothing, just as a price/earnings ratio, on a stand-alone basis, is completely useless. In deciding that Pfizer is cheap, what are those pundits measuring it against? The stock market as a whole? The average valuation of other pharmaceutical stocks? Pundits can gloss over this; you can't afford to, because you need a compelling reason to buy (or sell) a particular security or asset, and that means understanding relative valuations. Are large-cap stocks more appealing than their small-cap counterparts and thus a good place to invest more of your portfolio? That is the kind of question the right metrics will help you to answer, just as they help me.

You also can't rely on any single valuation tool in isolation. The ever-popular P/E ratio is the best example of this. Back in late September 1987, the S&P 500 stock index traded at 22 times actual earnings for the previous 12 months, while midway through the summer of 2002, it traded at 30 times earnings for the previous 12 months. Does that mean that stocks were a better bet in late September 1987 than they were in July 2002? Hardly. After all, the S&P plunged 30% in a single day in October 1987, whereas 2002 turned out to be the beginning of a long-lived stock market advance that would lead to a big jump in the S&P the following year. A superficial analysis looking only at absolute valuation would have ignored the factors that went into compiling price/earnings ratios. In 2002, for instance, P/E ratios were inflated artificially by the losses or tiny profits companies had reported in the midst of the recession (as well as the interest rate environment). It is interest rates that link earnings and prices; higher interest rates tend to drive P/E ratios lower, whereas in lower interest-rate environments, price/earnings ratios have room to grow. All things being equal, higher interest rates push the value of an income stream (whether bond income or dividend yield) lower.

A useful way to put the P/E ratio to work in the quest for the best valuation opportunities is to track the relative P/Es of one market compared to another over a period of time. If the P/E ratio of market A has tended to trade at a 10% premium to that of market B over the past 20 years, and now it trades at a discount, or at only a 5% premium, that tells me that market A may look relatively attractive on a valuation basis. As I write this, we are in the aftermath of a period during which the Russell 2000 Index (a great benchmark for small-cap stocks) has outpaced the S&P 500 for the past 5 years, generating nearly double the returns for investors. Not surprisingly, the P/E ratios of small-cap stocks trade at a significant premium to those of large-cap stocks; the kind of valuation disparity I haven't experienced since 1997. Monitoring this comparative data led me to rebalance small- and large-cap stocks in favor of large-cap stocks in the second quarter of 2007. A wise move; in the 2 years that have followed, the S&P trounced the Russell 2000.

Of course, these valuation relationships are subject to change over time. Back in the 1980s, when what pundits today refer to as "emerging markets" were more typically described as "underdeveloped countries," the valuation gap between the handful of stocks that traded on the fledgling stock exchanges in countries such as Mexico was wide enough to drive a truck through. Although that gap has shrunk over time as those emerging markets have become more numerous, more liquid, more diversified, and better regulated, trying to identify valuation opportunities based on history becomes more difficult. These days, the "risk premium" that had traditionally been applied to emerging market stocks has nearly vanished. Does that mean the emerging markets offer scanty investment opportunities, based on relative valuation? Perhaps—or maybe not. Perhaps it means that it's time for us to revamp our ideas of how to view valuation tools that are based on historical patterns, and supplement them with other metrics. Momentum metrics prove particularly useful in gauging whether valuation data is off-kilter or not. If it ever really is "different this time," we need to be flexible enough to adjust it. If your valuation metrics are steering you the wrong way, momentum will serve as a kind of guardrail, catching you before you drive off the cliff. (In other words, you'll experience "negative momentum," or lose money.) Momentum metrics are great insurance against massive and costly investment mistakes. Every once in a while, market relationships do change, and it truly becomes "different this time." This view, in my opinion, does not apply to the emerging markets. They're simply expensive.

Let's say, however, that your initial valuation analysis has led you to favor adding income-oriented investments like bonds or real estate to your portfolio rather than stocks. Now you'll need a different set of tools to measure the relative value of different parts of the global fixed-income markets. Despite my background as a bond investor, I have to remind myself that measuring bond yields holds its own set of challenges and perils. These bonds could be sovereign bonds issued by another country's government, junk bonds sold to finance a corporate buyout, or a bond pegged to a package of assets such as mortgages or credit card receivables. Any of these categories could hold hidden risk for which I, as an investor, would want to be compensated. The key valuation consideration for all of these is how much they yield, and once again, that has to be measured on a relative basis. Typically, U.S. investors in search of some kind of benchmark against which to measure the yields of potential fixed-income investments will turn to the Treasury bond market, recognizing that Treasurys offer the combination of the highest credit quality (a triple-A credit rating) and greatest liquidity. Treasury bonds are also issued with a wide array of maturity dates, making it relatively simple to find a comparable Treasury security to use as a benchmark for nearly any competing fixed-income instrument.

Whenever you delve into the world of bond investing, you end up grappling with the issue of credit risk. What are the odds that the issuer of these bonds is going to be able and willing to keep making the interest payments as promised, and repay the principal when it comes due in 5 or 10 years' time? In the world of the U.S. Treasury, those odds are pretty good. After all, the Treasury bills, notes, and bonds issued are backed by the "full faith and credit" of the U.S. government. Bond investors often joke that if the U.S. government ever defaults on these obligations, we'll all have a lot more to worry about than simply losing money; such a default would signal a national catastrophe. That's why professional investors use Treasury securities as a valuation benchmark and express the extra return they expect in exchange for the extra risk they take by venturing further afield in terms of the difference in yield between the Treasury and that new security: the yield spread. Let's suppose that you're contemplating investing in either a portfolio of emerging markets government bonds or a portfolio of bonds issued by U.S. companies with a mediocre, low triple-B credit rating. Both portfolios are made up of bonds that mature in 10 years, and, for the sake of argument, both carry the same credit rating. To figure out the better value, most investors will just calculate the current yield on both portfolios, and then compare those two figures to the yield on the 10-year Treasury. All things being equal, the portfolio that has the highest "spread" over the Treasury security is the one that offers the most attractive valuation: The bigger the spread, the higher the yield, and the more the investor is being paid for taking on the additional risk of venturing beyond the safe haven of the Treasury market.

The importance of credit risk was highlighted in the subprime crisis that began in the spring of 2007. As investors became more skittish, risk aversion ripped through the financial markets throughout the second half of that year and into 2008. By the end of November 2008, the crisis of confidence had escalated to the point that credit spreads resembled those seen only at the peaks of prior financial crises. Investors, it seems, were slapping a massive "distrust" premium on any investment that isn't a Treasury-backed security. That, in turn, raised the bar on the kinds of returns that stocks must appear to offer investors. When yields on bonds—which rank above stocks in a company's capital structure and thus offer a greater degree of security—soar to such generous levels, why take the extra risk of investing in stocks?

Some investors may be willing to invest in depreciating assets in exchange for a current income flow. For instance, an investor may decide to buy a video rental business despite the advent of Netflix and the ability to download movies directly from iTunes and other Internet sites. On the surface, it would seem that a video rental business has very little inherent value: At the very least, it's a wasting asset as these new business models displace the neighborhood store. Anyone making this bet, therefore, needs to be confident that the income it generates will produce more than 100% of the return: It is unlikely that the business can be sold at a profit. Sometimes this kind of investment does make sense, but you need to make the right kind of valuation calculation. In another example, you might want to invest in an oil well, even though it will eventually run dry and the mineral rights on the land will have no value. But in this case, you know that when you try to determine the well's investment value you need to focus on how much income that oil well will generate for you during its productive life. That may involve calculating how much oil is likely to be pumped out of the well (the well's reserves), and then how much that oil may fetch on the open market. Then you can decide whether the valuation proposition makes sense: whether the income from the oil well will exceed its purchase price by enough to make the return attractive relative to other potential investments.

Other investments offer little in the way of income. That house in Miami that you're thinking of buying? Unless it's a holiday home that you will rent out for 6 months out of every year, it's not going to generate any return until you decide to sell it. Similarly, an investor who buys gold as an investment will have to rely on metrics that rely only on capital appreciation; gold doesn't pay any dividends or generate other income. Indeed, some kinds of gold investing actually *cost* investors money (in storage and insurance costs for bullion, for instance), so the potential capital appreciation has to be large enough to offset that extra expense. Another example is venture capital funds, or an investment in promising but still-risky biotech companies. In both cases, returns will come if, and only if, the ideas and concepts are proven over time. Access to capital may become a "valuation fundamental"; so, too, may the Food and Drug Administration's decision whether to grant approval to a new drug.

Your job as an investor is to go beyond looking at the price you must pay for an investment you are contemplating and find a way to establish a value on it. Then, you must compare that value to the prevailing market price, as well as to the values and prices of other investment options. In some markets, that process will be relatively straightforward thanks to the existence of well-established metrics. In other cases, you might have to be creative. The objective is to develop a set of valuation metrics that can serve as a solid foundation for your entire investment process. If you don't understand how valuation metrics work and how to use them, you will hinder your own ability to assemble all the pieces of the investment puzzle and decipher what it is telling you.

12

Putting It Together

By this point, your head is probably spinning. You're thinking to your-self, what is this guy talking about? He's giving me a piece of data here, you mutter, another over there, but all I *really* need is a quick and easy formula along with a user's manual; *something* that will make tumultuous financial markets click into focus.

Believe me, I feel your pain (and that is more than just words). You're going through exactly what I suffered when I began trying to read the market's mind decades ago. Because I wasn't just managing my own finances but was responsible for the retirement savings and financial well-being of thousands of clients, I knew that I had to find a way to address that confusion. The methodology that I have just outlined for you is the result of years of trial and the occasional error. This methodology has been a valuable way for me to impose at least a degree of order on the chaos that the financial markets can appear to be. Constructing a robust investment process such as this is a bit like building a new house, one that won't let in the rain or snow, will with-stand earthquakes and high winds, and will be comfortable to live in. What I have done so far is steer you to the right materials to build this new house: the investment equivalents of, say, bricks, mortar, copper pipes for the plumbing, and wooden joists. But when you build a house, you need architectural plans to tell you how deep the founda-tions need to be, how to appropriately support the second story, where to put the fireplace and chimneys, and so on. Similarly, when you construct an investment process, you need not only the right materials to help you make decisions (the metrics that make up each of the five factors that I've shared with you), but also a plan that enables you to use that data in the right way. Thanks to the Internet, you have at your fingertips more information than any other generation in history. Now it's time to take a step back and look at the bigger picture: *How on earth, with so much potentially useful data to draw on, should you go about selecting which tool to use at any given time?*

Just as we all want to live in a house that corresponds to our own needs and preferences (one builder may need a home office; another, extra bedrooms to accommodate five children; a third, a self-contained apartment where the grandparents can live independently within the family), so everyone's specific investment needs will differ. Similarly, this kind of global macro decision making needs to take place within the context of a well thought-out strategic asset-allocation plan that takes into account your specific return objectives, cash flow and liquidity needs, and risk tolerance. Only then can you judge which investment decisions and market shifts will have the greatest impact on your own portfolio. That is why a recipe that works for me or works for my clients may not be the right one for you, in your specific investment circumstances. Providing you with a "one size fits all" formula, while you may heave a sigh of relief today, would be doing you a disservice in the long run. I will react to the same metrics differently than you do, and that is just as it should be, because my goals and considerations are different from yours. Equally, the way that I respond to a given situation in managing my personal "point and click" trading portfolio is likely to vary from the decisions I make with respect to the broader funds that I run on behalf of others. So, although I can give you the tools and even some hints about how to design the right kind of plan, ultimately the final decisions are in your hands. This is the point at which investing becomes as much of an art as it is a science.

I can, however, steer you in the direction of some broad guidelines or strategies. Still, before doing so, I need to remind you of the myriad ways that your emotions will conspire against you in your efforts to use metrics to "read" the financial markets. We've already discussed some of these in detail earlier in this book, such as the psychological comfort that comes from being part of a crowd. In the spring of 1999, for instance, the Fed funds valuation metric was telling me loud and clear that it was time to lighten up on stocks. Doing so, however, meant I would have had to break ranks with my peers—never an easy thing to do or to explain. Of course, with 20/20 hindsight, the signal was absolutely accurate—and a 3-year slump began less than a year later—but at the time this was the only metric giving me a definite indication that stocks were overvalued and poised for a selloff. Indeed, other metrics were telling us *not* to panic, giving me a reason to stay invested and remain in my comfort zone. Market momentum was strong; investor sentiment was robust, with Investors Intelligence reporting that bulls outnumbered bears by a ratio of two to one, and Treasury market metrics suggesting economic conditions were improving. I fretted about the decision. Which metrics should I trust? Like any other Chicago Cubs fan, I enjoy sitting in a ballpark among thousands of like-minded people, cheering my team on. But just because I'm going to cheer them on doesn't mean I'm irrational enough to risk my hard-earned capital (or that of my investors) betting on the risky proposition that they may, after more than a century, make it all the way to a World Series. Especially when at least one key indicator was flashing a warning sign. By the late summer of 1999, more metrics were coming into line with the core valuation signal and were giving me more confidence that my judgment to lighten up on stocks had been correct. Although the stock market was still advancing, fewer stocks contributed to each new high, and the yield curve was flattening.

It's easy to look back in time at a big turning point like that one. What you will find, as I have, is that applying a metrics-based process to the investment decisions you need to make today and tomorrow requires not only confidence but hard work and patience. To start with, not every turning point is as dramatic as that of 1999, so we all need to pay attention to the subtlest signals that financial markets emit in order to boost the odds of long-term outperformance. That's why I study the metrics that make up each of these five factors every day of the week. It is why every day, every week, and every month I review my asset allocation in light of any changes and stand ready to recommend changing our weighting in any asset class or category depending on what those metrics tell me.

This is where we confront one more human foible: impatience. If what you are looking for is a simple, clear-cut recipe for investment success, I'm afraid you're about to be disappointed. If I told you that whenever the price/earnings ratio of large-cap stocks creeps above x you need to take a teaspoon of psychology and mix it with 2 cups of valuation and a half-cup of momentum to get a clear buy or sell signal, I'd be selling you a bill of goods. Using factors is all about taking time to study and think about them; it's about using judgment. Any game, whether it's old maid or chess, comes with rules that players have to learn. But any moderately intelligent person can triumph at hearts after a few hours, whereas winning at chess or bridge—like "winning" in investing—requires an extra edge: strategic thinking. Of course, just as bidding conventions in bridge and acknowledged game openings or strategies in chess exist, there are some rules of thumb when it comes to the kind of quantitative-based global macro investment process I am urging you to devise. For instance, it's generally a good plan to put your spare cash to work in a market that looks cheap in absolute and relative terms and that already seems to be moving in the right direction. But the key to strategic thinking is a kind of sixth sense that should be added to these five factors. Only time and a greater familiarity with the metrics that comes from using them will tell you when it's time to ignore what one factor appears to be signaling, when to emphasize what another set of metrics is telling you, or when you need to give a greater weight than you have historically to another factor.

Let me show you some of the ways that different factors can work together, or conflict, in a real-life scenario that probably is still clear in your memory. Let's go back to the aftermath of the bear market of 2000 to 2002, when all professional investors were eagerly awaiting signs that the market was about to begin a long-awaited recovery. Just as it had been hard for even risk-averse investors to abandon the bull market in late 1999, thinking of investing during the agonizing summer of 2002 was painful with the collapse of Enron and WorldCom fresh in our minds and the headlines. Nonetheless, by June 2002, I was champing at the bit. I knew that keeping an outsize position in bonds and remaining dramatically underweight in stocks wasn't a tenable strategy for long-term outperformance. Keeping in mind that the first and most significant decision investors can or should make is how to divide their portfolio between stocks and bonds, I was waiting for the five factors to tell me when the moment of maximum opportunity and minimal risk had arrived. Only then could I take the next step and start exploring which segments of the stock market offered the best opportunities.

As I've pointed out, valuation is the lynchpin for any investment process. A compelling valuation argument must be in place for the portfolio structure you build to rest on solid foundations. So, if you're looking for signs that large-cap stocks are about to outperform, turn to valuation metrics. Is the prospective earnings yield on the S&P 500 (the barometer of large-cap stocks) at least as rosy as that for the yield on an index of triple-B bonds? (Check any of the many available data sources for this information. To calculate the earnings yield, just take the forward price/earnings ratio on the S&P 500 and flip the numbers so that a P/E ratio of 14 becomes a 1/14th for a percentage of 7.14%.) If the fundamental metrics are sending encouraging signals, you can move on to other key factors, such as the economy: Is it expanding or contracting? Economic metrics that we have already discussed, such as the yield curve, should give you some clues. Cue the next factor: liquidity. How much dry powder is available in the market, and how great is the tolerance for risk? Again, looking at metrics will tell us how much capital is sitting on the sidelines; credit spreads will give us clues to how much investors want to be paid for taking on more risk, as spelled out in the pages of *Barron's,* which tracks the spread between yields on intermediate-grade and top-tier bonds. (An additional tip: Downloading a decade's worth of this data into a spreadsheet will give you a solid historical basis for comparison.) Now you can take a look at the fourth factor: market sentiment, or investor psychology. Use metrics to take the market's emotional temperature: Are investors complacent or fearful? Finally, momentum, the factor that, in many ways, stands shoulder to shoulder with valuation as vital in shaping an investment decision. If valuation is giving you a green light but momentum metrics are telling you equally urgently that hitting the "buy" button would be dangerous, you need to watch out. Once momentum falls into place and all five factors align, it's a beautiful thing.

Watching the market in the summer of 2002, all five factors did seem to be forming an encouraging pattern. By June, the S&P 500 had lost 18% over the course of the previous 12 months, enough to bring the forward earnings yield on the S&P 500 back above that on the 10-year Treasury note. The Fed model was telling me, loud and clear, that large-cap stocks were now more than 5% undervalued. It was the buy signal for which I had been waiting. But I still wanted the other factors to confirm that it was time to act on that green light, and the critical one—momentum—wasn't obliging. Market breadth, measured by the ratio of the number of stocks advancing to those declining, kept telling me that the market was stuck in a funk. The result was a stalemate.

Whenever that happens, and especially whenever a crucial turning point may be at hand, (something that only happens a few times in a decade), I turn to the secondary factors and dig more deeply into the metrics there to see what they tell me. By the middle of 2002, the bear market had taken a toll on investors' psyches, and bears outnumbered bulls by two to one. By December, with the key valuation metric egging me on by reminding me that large-cap stocks were now 30% undervalued, bearishness was growing, and market sentiment was also pointing in the same direction. All that I needed to tell me that it was safe to jump back into the stock market, I concluded, was a positive reading on the momentum front. That came at last in March 2003, when the market's breadth began to improve. At last, more stocks were advancing than declining in any given trading session. A month later, the S&P 500 climbed more than 4 percentage points above its 200-day moving average. At last: an attractive entry point! I recommended being underweight to overweight in stocks in clients' portfolios, and over the next 12 months watched the S&P soar 23%.

I'm not suggesting that catching the end of the 2008 bear market will be simple or straightforward. But using metrics in this way—carefully, with patience and discipline—you will be able to feel your way back into stocks when the time is right, whether that is on the day you first read this or perhaps not for another two or three years. At some point, it will become clear to you, reading the signals that metrics are sending, that investing still more in the safe haven of Treasury securities will amount to investing in an overpriced market. Whenever a particularly dramatic rally or selloff has occurred, as happened during the fourth quarter of 2008, it's particularly important to monitor metrics. It is during the times when the upside/downside risk is less visible that discipline and strategic thinking come into play. To be successful—to capture or at least be aware of all the potential investment opportunities on a global macro basis—you need a process that reviews all your options on a regular basis, even when you're not looking for an entry point into a depressed market or a clue that it's time to take your money out of one that you already suspect is significantly overvalued. In other words, you need a disciplined approach.

Although there is no one-size-fits-all investment process, you should apply some rules of thumb when studying and using metrics to reach an investment decision, whether you're contemplating a major asset-allocation shift or simply undertaking a routine review.

Think about what the metrics *appear* to be telling you. Don't accept the signals they appear to be sending without question or further thought. In early 2006, the yield curve inverted: Suddenly, the yields on the shorter-term Treasury securities were higher than those on longer-dated Treasury notes. This time around, however, the yield curve inversion reflected a global liquidity rush as trading partners in the emerging markets (notably China) parked their surplus in U.S. Treasury securities, distorting the yields on those Treasurys.

What might be happening in the financial markets that isn't yet showing up in the metrics (for one reason or another)? Are the metrics telling you the *whole* truth? In the immediate aftermath of the September 11 terrorist attacks, investors weren't reacting only to events but to the atmosphere of uncertainty that those events had created. What would the fallout be from another terrorist attack? That kind of hour-to-hour uncertainty translated into a lack of trust in the authorities, ranging from political leaders to corporate CEOs, a lack of trust that later disclosures of corporate malfeasance at companies such as Enron seemed to validate. Most important from the perspective of an investor, it translated into an absolute and utter risk aversion. Investors may not have been able to control what the terrorists might do next and the risks linked to terrorism, but they could control whether they invested capital in the financial markets. Not surprisingly, they sat on their cash. In that environment, traditional liquidity metrics didn't reflect fundamentals.

Ask yourself whether there are new metrics available that might provide a better picture of the investment landscape. The world is in a state of flux. New markets emerge that behave in new and different ways, and tried-and-true metrics may give way to new and improved quantitative tools. Years ago, for instance, measuring equity mutual fund cash balances as a percentage of total equity mutual fund assets was a useful liquidity metric. These cash balances theoretically represented money available to be put to work in the market (and could thus fuel a future rally). As investors flocked to index funds, however, mutual fund managers trying to beat an index couldn't afford to let much cash sit idle for long. Monitoring cash balances became obsolete because the data point no longer had any real significance; the fact that they were low had little or nothing to do with how managers viewed market valuations or opportunity.

Are you keeping an eye open for even the most unlikely or unexpected possibilities? Sometimes that means battling your preconceptions. Commodities, for instance, are an asset class that has for decades at a time languished on the sidelines. Unlike stocks or bonds, owning gold, oil, or copper futures doesn't generate any cash flow or dividends. (Indeed, thanks to the structure of these markets, anyone who wants to maintain a position in commodities has to pay for the privilege.) It's hard to monitor fundamentals: No entity such as Gold Corp. or Copper Inc. reports quarterly profits or losses and discusses risk factors in filings with the Securities and Exchange Commission. Therefore, figuring out the "fair value" of a commodity itself (rather than a mining company, say) may be nearly impossible. When it comes to gold, a commodity whose value lies strictly in the eye of the beholder and that has very few industrial uses, the task is even trickier. And yet, bypassing commodities isn't the answer, either. While the period from December 1986 through November 2007 saw a measly 2.3% annualized return for the Commodity Research Bureau's index of spot commodity prices (compared to 11.4% for the S&P 500 and 7.7% for bonds), at times throughout that period investors who spotted temporary supply/demand imbalances could have made a lot of money, particularly in the bull market of 2003 to 2007.

Just because familiar metrics aren't there or don't work in a familiar way doesn't always mean that an asset class is a bad idea. Over a 5-month period in 2001, the Federal Reserve slashed its key lending rates, bringing the Fed Funds rate and its companion interest rate down to 3.5% from 6.5%. The goal was to fight off a potential recession; the result was a clear buy signal for commodities. But the thought of adding commodities to private client accounts was unusual, to say the least. If I was going to go out on this limb, all five factors needed to be in alignment, I decided. But despite the growing importance of commodities to many investors, the market had only three useful sets of metrics: the relationship between the Fed Funds rate and the consumer inflation rate, the 200-day moving average of an index, and the breadth of any index move. That's it. I would have to find a way to rely on what I would normally consider to be inadequate data. Ultimately, in March 2002, the Dow Jones AIG-Commodity Index finally climbed more than 4 percentage points above its 200-day moving average. At last the commodities market's fundamentals seemed positive, in both absolute and relative terms, *and* the momentum indicators were in place. Thankfully, at about the same time, PIMCO, a global investment management firm, introduced their Commodity Real Return Fund, so gaining access to commodities became as easy as buying mutual fund shares at just the right point in time. As a result, we recommended a portion of client portfolios be allocated to commodities, and over the next 4 years we generated annualized returns of 16.7% from this move in a period when the S&P earned a much more modest 9.3% on an annualized basis. We closed out those positions in 2006 when the commodities index fell more than 4% below its 200-day moving average and as Federal Reserve policy makers began to raise interest rates once more.

What asset class do I sell to generate cash to invest in the commodities market if I spot another opportunity there? And when I sell an investment, where do I direct the proceeds? Almost as important as the investment decision itself is the origin of the proceeds used to fund the investment. Sometimes the ultimate source or use of funds can be as challenging as the investment itself. In the absence of any terminology devoted to this tricky subject, a veteran investor and friend of mine, Ron Laughlin, once dubbed the asset class or securities purchased with the proceeds of a sale a "gazinta," a nonsense word derived from the phrase *goes into* (as in, "what the proceeds go into"). For the most part, you won't need to resort to nonsense words like that. The metrics, if you calculate them properly and use them consistently, will offer you a cool and unbiased view of the relative merits of each investment option. Ultimately, however, the answer will hinge on your personal attitudes and circumstances—and it's one point where it's appropriate to consider your own biases, such as your tolerance of risk. You might conclude that this global macro approach to investing is appropriate for only part of your portfolio, where you are comfortable making gradual shifts in asset allocation. If you are concerned about the tax consequences of making portfolio changes, you may decide to limit your active asset-allocation decisions to portfolios sheltered from taxes, specifically retirement accounts such as IRAs and 401(k)s. (Alternatively, you might be a more aggressive investor with a longer-term horizon and less tax sensitivity and thus more comfortable with making frequent, larger allocation shifts, including style tilts across the entirety of your portfolio.) Suppose that all five factors agree that stocks look pricey. One investor might react by slashing his allocation to stocks and even establishing a short position that would allow him to profit from future declines in a major market index. Another might simply decide to take some extra cash that might otherwise have been allocated to buying stocks over a period of time and direct it toward another asset class instead, leaving her core holdings untouched. The two approaches will result in different returns and incur a different degree of risk. Both, however, fall under the broad outlines of my factor-based approach to investing, and both are equally appropriate as long as the investors have considered carefully their personal circumstances as well as what the factors say about the investment environment

But, I can almost hear you ask, aren't there some rules of thumb associated with the five factors that apply to all investors? Absolutely. So the first question always to ask yourself is whether stocks look like a safe and attractive investment, relative to your other options, whatever those may be. Indeed, given the long-term tendency of stocks to outperform bonds (as noted at the beginning of this analysis, over the past 18 years, stocks have delivered annualized returns of about

10.5%, compared to 8% annualized returns from bonds), any investor with a long time horizon should consider an equity-oriented portfolio. (True, stocks have been a horrible place to be for the past decade as a whole—but during multiyear periods during that decade, they have fared well...hence the importance of monitoring your portfolio constantly.) The reason to include bonds in the mix is the fact that most of us don't have a multidecade investment horizon. But only after you've decided how much of your portfolio you can allocate to stocks, based on your personal risk tolerance, return objectives, and other circumstances, can you decide how to divide up that allocation. Once you have decided that the entire stock market universe, domestic or international, looks appealing based on the five factors, you can drill down one step. Convention and common sense dictate that we should compare any alternative stock investment to the ultra-liquid bellwether of the S&P 500. What do factors such as fundamentals, momentum, and psychology tell you about small-cap stocks, on that relative basis? Or emerging markets? You can use the five factors to tell you where the "sweet spot" is *within* the global stock market universe just as you did when evaluating an entry or exit point to stocks as a whole, or when comparing stocks to bonds or commodities. Repeatedly, valuation and momentum emerge as the most important of these five factors, whether you are trying to understand whether growth or value stocks appear most attractive or if you should be overweighting large-cap stocks at the expense of their smaller peers.

Can metrics identify turning points within asset classes as well as between them? Metrics are useful whenever you need to measure the absolute or relative attractions of any group of investments. I have found studying the five factors very helpful in navigating one of the most basic decisions: whether and when to shift money from large-cap stocks to small-caps, or vice versa. At the beginning of 2007, the Russell 2000 Index, a benchmark of smaller stocks, had just wrapped up a 6-year stretch during which its components soared 76%, compared to a gain of 19% for the S&P 500, the large-cap stock benchmark. Valuations were so extreme that everyone knew it was only a matter of time before the small-cap rally sputtered to a halt. Not surprisingly, I was glued to my models and anxiously watching all five factors, looking for them to align in telling me that it was finally time to reduce or eliminate my exposure to small caps. The valuation picture was clear, and the psychology part of the picture was taking shape, too. The momentum factor finally kicked in during the first week of July 2007, when the Russell's return relative to the S&P 500 slipped below the 10-month moving average, and my team and I responded by recommending that we shift a portion of our small-cap stock allocation over to larger stocks.

Making timely allocations like that is what all the metrics that collectively make up the five factors are all about. Navigating the financial markets is never simple or straightforward, as the events of 2008 reminded us all too clearly. Globalization adds one level of complexity, the proliferation of new investment products and new strategies another. Today, investors in Boise can purchase Mexican pesos or Thai infrastructure stocks as readily as they can a large-cap U.S. index fund, or could opt instead to snap up an exchange-traded fund based on alternative fuels. Each new investment opportunity brings with it the potential for success in the shape of a few percentage points of additional return each year. As baby boomers head toward retirement, that extra smidgen could spell, cumulatively, the difference between a comfortable retirement with few financial worries and one where an unexpected surge in gasoline prices knocks your budget off kilter. For younger investors, or those whose assets are large enough that they have few financial worries, the challenge is different. How can they winnow through the constantly expanding opportunity set in search of the best combination of risk and return?

Complexity can be a good thing, especially when it comes to investment opportunities (at least for those with the ability to manage that complexity). Some investors will need only guidance on when to buy and sell—how to identify when the risk-adjusted returns in various markets look most compelling. Others will need more help in managing their portfolios. All, however, will benefit by constructing an investment process firmly rooted in the conviction that a successful portfolio is one based on analysis rather than hunches, emotions, and tips. Moreover, basing that process on quantitative tools means that anyone can find any part of the market more understandable.

The metrics that we have explored and discussed in this book, and which collectively make up the five factors on which I base my own investment model, are just tools. They are available to all investors to use creatively to answer the questions that preoccupy and perplex them the most. I might ponder the small-cap/large-cap asset-allocation question, because that is the most pressing issue for me and my clients. But you can use the same factors to consider whether Indian or Chinese stocks offer the best way to "play" the emerging markets story. One thing is certain: We'll all be looking for the signs that the stock market rout of 2008 will reverse itself...

The universe of investment opportunities is so immense that as long as you are only following someone else's footsteps on the ground, you will never be able to appreciate it, much less seize the opportunities it offers. Only by taking to the sky and looking down at the investment landscape can you begin to deploy these metrics in your search for the ideal place to put your capital. From my own view 30,000 feet off the ground, the view is always enticing.

INDEX

A

active asset allocation in global macro
strategy, 23
adjusting data, 69
advance/decline ratio, momentum
and, 107-110
AIG, liquidity problems of, 135
American Association of Individual
Investors, 161
annual returns, estimating range
of, 16
asset allocation, 5
active allocation, 23
tactical allocation, 39
asset classes, turning points
within, 200

B

Barron's, sentiment indicator in,
161-162
bear market of 2000-2002 example,
193-194
Bed Bath & Beyond example, 32
benchmarks for metrics, 69-72
Berkshire Hathaway, 176
Bernanke, Ben, 146
Berns, Gregory, 158
bias in metrics, 75
"big liquidity," 144-147
Black Monday (Oct. 19, 1987),
emotional reactions to, 51
bond market example (fundamental
valuations), 174-175, 185-186

breadth (of market), 107-110
BRIC countries (Brazil, Russia, India,
China), 74
Buffett, Warren, 42, 176
Business Week cover story, effect on
market psychology, 159

C

Canadian oil sands junket, 31
casual versus causal relationships,
76-78
CDOs (collateralized debt
obligations), 62
central banks, effect on liquidity,
144-147
Claussen, Ron, 87
closed-end mutual funds
liquidity and, 142-143
open-end mutal funds versus, 46
Clusius, Carolus, 15
collateralized debt obligations
(CDOs), 62
commodities, 197-198
momentum and, 104
Conference Board's Composite Index
of Leading Indicators, 128
context in metrics, 75-78
contradictory signals, handling, 89-92
contrarian indicators, 164
conviction, power of, 54
corporate profits, relationship with
stock prices, 118
correlation, 76-78

FINANCIAL TIMES

In an increasingly competitive world, it is quality
of thinking that gives an edge—an idea that opens new
doors, a technique that solves a problem, or an insight
that simply helps make sense of it all.

We work with leading authors in the various arenas
of business and finance to bring cutting-edge thinking
and best-learning practices to a global market.

It is our goal to create world-class print publications
and electronic products that give readers
knowledge and understanding that can then be
applied, whether studying or at work.

To find out more about our business
products, you can visit us at www.ftpress.com.